Wild Rice Star of the North

150 Minnesota Recipes for a Gourmet Grain

THE 1006 SUMMIT AVENUE SOCIETY

McGRAW-HILL BOOK COMPANY

New York   St. Louis   San Francisco   Toronto
Hamburg   Mexico

1 2 3 4 5 6 7 8 9 S E M S E M 8 7 6 5

ISBN 0-07-002455-3

Library of Congress Cataloging in Publication Data

Main entry under title:
Wild rice, star of the north.

1. Cookery (Wild rice)   2. Cookery—Minnesota.
I. 1006 Summit Avenue Society.
TX809.W55W55 1985   641.6'318   85-6684
ISBN 0-07-002455-3

Cover drawings, illustrations,
and calligraphy by Mary M. McKee

Contents

Dear Readers:

This cookbook represents a marriage of two projects of great importance to me as the spouse of the Governor of Minnesota.

Traveling throughout the world, I have enjoyed telling others about wild rice, Minnesota's official state grain. Our state is the world leader in wild rice production, so it is a long-standing Minnesota product that is also delicious and nutritious. A wild-rice cookbook seemed like a wonderful way to promote greater use of this grain.

This cookbook also presented an opportunity to raise funds for another project in which I have great interest— the much-needed restoration of the Governor's Residence, one of the most historically and architecturally significant homes on St. Paul's magnificent Summit Avenue.

Wild rice has come a long way from its origins as a staple for the native Americans who first populated our state. Today it is featured in most fine restaurants. Because of its unique flavor and appealing texture, it is appreciated by many as a delicacy. Like many Minnesotans, the Governor and I enjoy presenting gifts of wild rice to friends at holidays, to visitors in Minnesota and to our hosts wherever we travel.

Although we like to call it the gourmet grain, wild rice is a festive part of our family fare. We hope these recipes help you enjoy this memorable Minnesota food often.

Sincerely,

Lola Perpich

OFFICERS OF THE
1006 SUMMIT AVENUE SOCIETY

The 1006 Summit Avenue Society is a nonprofit fund-raising organization devoted to help preserve, maintain and restore the Minnesota Governor's Residence. Lola Perpich, wife of Governor Rudy Perpich, asked the Society to produce a wild rice cookbook which would generate interest in and promote this native Minnesota product. Proceeds from *Wild Rice, Star of the North* will add to the funds for preservation, restoration and renovation of one of our state's most significant homes.

This house was given to the state by the Horace Hills Irvine family to be used as a home for the incumbent Governor. It has become a symbol of warmth and hospitality reflecting the many aspects of our state's development and its history.

We hope you will thoroughly enjoy this collection of wild rice lore and recipes gathered from kitchens throughout Minnesota.

THE 1006 SUMMIT AVENUE SOCIETY

Wild Rice

Wild rice (Zizania aquatica) *is an aquatic grass native to the central and Upper Great Lakes region of the United States, and is not related to the common rice* (Oryza sativa).

From *The Song of Hiawatha*

Unmolested worked the women,
Made their sugar from the maple
Gathered wild rice in the meadows . . .
Then Nokomis the old woman
Spoke and said to Minnehaha:
'Tis the moon when leaves are falling
All the wild rice has been gathered . . .

—HENRY WADSWORTH LONGFELLOW

Introduction

WILD RICE FACTS

Wild rice, often called the "gourmet grain," has been a staple in the diet of the Chippewa and Sioux Indian tribes for hundreds of years. *Mahnomen,* the Chippewa name for wild rice, comes from the words "mano," meaning good, and "min," meaning grain or berry, and it is indeed a good grain! It was so important to the Indians' lives that for several hundred years tribal wars were waged for control of the shallow lakes and rivers where this nutritious grain flourished. Indian tribes whose diets included wild rice were taller and stronger and survived the winters better than those who did not have a supply.

In the seventeenth century when the first white men, fur traders and explorers, came to the upper midwest region of the United States, they became acquainted with wild rice. The French called it *folle avoine*, which translates to crazy or wild oats. Later, they changed the name to wild rice because the similarity of the culture reminded them of white rice.

Not Really a Rice

Wild rice is not really a rice at all but rather an aquatic grass seed. It is the state grain of Minnesota—the only grain native to the North American continent.

Growing and Harvesting

Wild rice is harvested in the early fall. Only about 20 percent is harvested in the traditional method using canoes in the wild rice-filled lakes and rivers. Harvested by using giant combines, the remaining annual supply of nearly 5 million pounds comes from man-made paddies. A relatively new industry, only about fifteen years old, the paddy production of wild rice has stabilized the supply, and to some extent, the price.

In the early 1980's, Minnesota became the largest producer of wild rice, growing nearly two-thirds of the world's supply. The Canadian provinces of Ontario, Manitoba and Saskatchewan are significant producers as well as California and Idaho.

The illustrations and methods of harvesting described in this book relate to the traditional methods used by native Americans for gathering wild rice from the lakes and rivers. Today, the natural stands of wild rice are harvested in much the same way, but are closely regulated by state or province Departments of Natural Resources. Processing is done by the age-old method used for small quantities of wild rice. At the present time only about 20% of the 5 million-pound harvest is gathered in the traditional method and an even smaller percent is Indian-processed. The majority of wild rice available in the market today is grown in man-made paddies and processed in modern plants.

COOKING WILD RICE

As it cooks, wild rice absorbs moisture into the grain kernels so they are tender. Color, size and moisture content of wild rice will affect the length of cooking time.

Color of Grain

Wild rice may vary from very dark, shiny grains to light-colored ones. The dark outer coat is very tough, making it difficult for water to penetrate. Therefore, in the processing of wild rice, this outer layer is scratched to allow liquid to be absorbed. This is called "scarifying." The more scarifying that is done, the lighter the color of the kernel, and the faster it will cook.

Size of Grain

Larger grains require longer cooking time than smaller grains because they take longer to absorb water. Of course, broken grains cook quite quickly.

A good share of the wild rice on the market today contains a small percentage of broken and uneven size grains. The bulk of any rice you buy will cook uniformly. Usually, this type of rice is less costly than the 100 percent whole grain and is suitable for use in all recipes.

Moisture Content

As wild rice is processed, the moisture content is reduced. It may vary from 7 percent to 10 percent moisture, depending on the processor. The lower the moisture, the longer it takes to cook.

Rinsing Wild Rice

Modern wild rice processing plants are very careful to package wild rice under sanitary conditions, so it does not need to be rinsed. However, to enhance its appearance, it may be rinsed without losing any food value, as the nutrients are located inside the grains, rather than near the surface.

The cloudy gray foam that appears when cooking unrinsed wild rice is not contamination or dirt, but rather part of the grain. As wild rice goes through the scarifying process, static electricity is generated, causing waste particles to stick to the wild-rice grains. These particles cannot be completely vacuumed away. That "dust" is merely part of the grain.

Using hot tap water to rinse wild rice before cooking speeds up the cooking process. Rinsing may be done by using a strainer and running water through the rice or by placing the rice in a pan, adding water and pouring it off. CAUTION: Pouring off any excess liquid after the wild rice is cooked, or even partially cooked, will result in the loss of some food value and some flavor; therefore, using a minimum amount of water in cooking is desirable.

Soaking

Wild rice may be soaked for several hours or overnight and it will shorten cooking time by a few minutes. Discarding the soaking water will not result in the loss of any nutrients.

Basic Cooking Directions

A note about package directions: Usually, packages of wild rice come with basic cooking directions. Following these directions, particularly as to cooking time, insures success since they have been developed especially for that particular brand of rice.

BASIC PROPORTIONS (to make 3 cups cooked wild rice)

1 cup uncooked wild rice
3 cups liquid (water, bouillon, broth, stock or wine or a combination)
$1/2$ teaspoon salt (optional)

STOVE-TOP METHOD

Combine wild rice, liquid and salt in a heavy saucepan; heat to boiling. Reduce heat, cover; simmer 30 minutes. Check for doneness. Continue simmering until tender, checking every 5 minutes. Wild rice usually cooks tender in 30 to 45 minutes, but occasionally, due to color, size and moisture content, it may vary.

OVEN METHOD

Combine wild rice, liquid and salt in a baking dish. Cover and bake at 325°F for $1^1/_4$ to $1^1/_2$ hours or until tender. This method is especially practical if the oven is already being used for another part of the meal.

MICROWAVE METHOD

Combine wild rice, water and salt in a microwave-safe dish. Cook on high power 5 minutes; then on 50 percent power 30 to 40 minutes. Cover to prevent excess evaporation.

TEST FOR DONENESS

Wild rice should be cooked for the minimum amount of time required to achieve a tender attractive product. The grains should be swollen and cracked down the side. Wild rice that is opened and turned back like popped corn is overcooked and has lost its identifying shape. Overcooking also results in loss of texture, color and flavor.

Because wild rice is a natural product, it often will cook a little unevenly; a few grains will be "wide open" or curled back before the majority are tender. Remove a few grains and bite into them to test for tenderness. After cooking wild rice a few times, you will begin to know when it is done just by looking at it.

A WORD ABOUT BASIC RECIPE RATIOS

Using a ratio of 3 parts liquid to 1 part wild rice will usually produce a cooked rice without need to drain off excess liquid. If there is liquid remaining using this ratio, try 2½ parts water to 1 part wild rice. Using a minimum amount of liquid, which can all be absorbed during cooking, avoids the loss of any nutrients through draining.

A WORD ABOUT SALT

Recent studies indicate that we should limit our intake of salt. Wild rice has a nutlike roasted flavor which can be enjoyed without adding salt. One-half teaspoon of salt per cup of wild rice has been suggested, but more or less can be used according to taste.

VARIATION OF FLAVOR

Use of beef or chicken broth, stock, bouillon or wine instead of water for cooking gives additional flavor and is desirable for wild rice which is to be used as a side dish, in soups or casseroles.

COOLING WILD RICE

Once the wild rice is cooked, allowing it to remain in a covered pan, even off the heat, may cause the rice to over-cook. If the rice is not to be used immediately, remove the cover and stir gently to dissipate some of the heat. Spreading the wild rice out in a large flat pan will also cool it quickly. If the wild rice is to be used in a cold salad or dessert, chill it.

STORING COOKED WILD RICE

Large amounts of wild rice can be prepared at one time and stored for future use. For short-term storage (up to two weeks), store in a covered container in the refrigerator. For longer storage, freeze. To thaw frozen wild rice quickly, place in a strainer and either run hot tap water through it or place over a steaming kettle. The wild rice will be ready to use in just a few minutes.

STORING UNCOOKED WILD RICE

Use the same precautions as with any grain or grain product. Store in tightly sealed containers in a cool, dark, dry place. Wild rice is low in fat and therefore not subject to becoming rancid. It is also low in moisture, which contributes to a long shelf life—even several years! Storing in the freezer is not necessary, but if circumstances are less than ideal, and space permits, freezer storage is all right.

Decorative containers which do not seal tightly are adequate for short-term storage. For larger quantities or long-term storage, follow the suggestions above.

Food Value

Wild rice is a good cereal protein, equal to oat groats, and has a considerably higher protein value than wheat. As with any cereal protein, wild rice is an incomplete protein and should be served with meat or other complete protein. Wild rice is also an excellent source for B vitamins and potassium. Low in fat and calories, one cup of cooked wild rice contains about 130 calories. Wild rice contains about the same quantity of crude fiber as brown rice and oats but half that of wheat and corn.

The USDA Agricultural Handbook No. 8, *Composition of Food*, gives this analysis of 3¼ ounces (100 grams or about ½ cup) of uncooked wild rice.

14.10 grams protein
339.0 grams phosphorus
.45 milligrams thiamine
.79 grams fat
4.20 milligrams iron
.63 milligrams riboflavin
75.00 grams carbohydrates
6.20 milligrams niacin
7.00 milligrams sodium
19.00 milligrams calcium
220.00 milligrams potassium

Yields

1 pound of wild rice contains about 2⅔ cups.
1 cup of uncooked wild rice yields about 3 cups cooked.
1 pound of wild rice makes 12 to 14 (⅔-cup) servings.

Appetizers & More

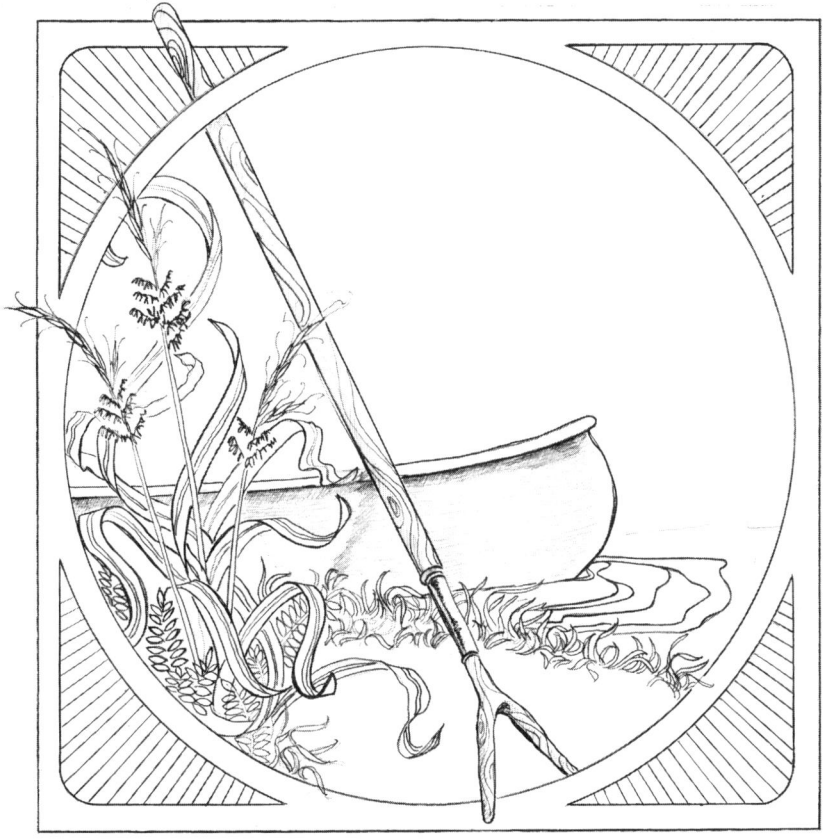

The canoe is the traditional type of boat used to gather wild rice from natural stands in lakes and rivers. It is propelled through the shallow waters with a forked pole. Present-day wild rice pickers use the same style of canoe, harvesting about 200 pounds of green rice per day.

Stuffed Baked Mushroom Caps

⅓ cup uncooked wild rice (1 cup cooked)

1 pound medium-size fresh mushrooms (about 24)

1 medium onion, very finely chopped

2 tablespoons herb butter*

5 slices bacon, crisply fried and crumbled

Parmesan cheese, freshly grated

Cook wild rice following one of basic methods (page xvi). Heat oven to 350°F. Clean mushrooms; remove stems. Finely chop stems; sauté with onion in herb butter. Stir in wild rice and bacon. Fill mushroom caps with stuffing mixture. Sprinkle with Parmesan cheese. Bake 15 to 20 minutes. Serve hot.

24 appetizers.

*For herb butter, combine 2 tablespoons softened butter with 1 teaspoon chopped parsley, ¼ teaspoon dried oregano and dash of garlic powder.

Spinach Wild Rice Pie

½ cup uncooked wild rice (1½ cups cooked)

2 (10-ounce) packages frozen chopped spinach, thawed

1½ cups chopped onion

¼ cup olive oil

6 eggs

1½ cups ricotta cheese

8 ounces feta cheese, crumbled

¾ cup chopped fresh dill weed

1 teaspoon freshly ground pepper

14 sheets frozen phyllo dough, thawed

1 cup butter or margarine, melted

Cook wild rice following one of basic methods (page xvi). Drain spinach very well; squeeze dry in strainer. Sauté onion in olive oil. Beat eggs in medium bowl; add wild rice, spinach, onion, cheeses, dill weed and pepper; mix well. Heat oven to 350°F. Unfold phyllo dough; keep leaves covered with damp towel to prevent drying. Separate one leaf; place in 15½ × 10½ × 1-inch jelly-roll pan; brush with melted butter. Repeat 6 more times. Spoon wild rice—spinach mixture over leaves. Layer 7 more leaves, brushing each leaf with melted butter. Trim edges of dough with scissors, if necessary. Bake 45 to 60 minutes or until browned. Cool; cut into 1½-inch squares.

60 appetizers.

VARIATION: Cut into large portions and serve as a side dish or luncheon main dish.

Chippewa Quiche

Wild rice adds a special flavor and texture to traditional quiche.

⅓ cup uncooked wild rice (1 cup cooked)

Pastry for 10-inch, one-crust pie

½ pound turkey ham, or regular ham, cut into ¼-inch cubes

8 ounces (about 2 cups) Swiss cheese shredded

2 tablespoons butter or margarine

3 green onions, including tops, minced

½ large green pepper, diced

4 eggs

1 cup whipping cream

Cook wild rice following one of basic methods (page xvi). Heat oven to 450°F. Prepare pastry and line 13 × 9 × 2-inch pan. Bake about 5 minutes. Remove from oven; cool pastry. Reduce oven temperature to 375°F. Sprinkle wild rice, ham and cheese in pastry shell. In small skillet, melt butter; add onions and green pepper. Cook and stir over medium-high heat until onions are soft, 3 to 4 minutes. Sprinkle over ingredients in pastry shell. Beat eggs and whipping cream together. Pour over mixture in pastry shell. Bake 35 to 45 minutes or until quiche is set. Cut into 1½-inch squares. Serve hot or cooled.

30 appetizers.

VARIATION: Can also be baked in a 10-inch pie plate and cut into wedges for a side dish or luncheon main dish.

6 servings.

Stuffed Endive

²/₃ cup uncooked wild rice (2 cups cooked)

About 3 heads Belgian endive

¹/₂ cup golden raisins

¹/₃ cup toasted, chopped pine nuts

¹/₃ cup mayonnaise

¹/₃ cup dairy sour cream

¹/₄ teaspoon curry powder

Cook wild rice following one of basic methods (page xvi); chill. Rinse and drain endive well; separate into leaves. Combine wild rice, raisins, pine nuts, mayonnaise, sour cream and curry powder; stuff into leaves. Refrigerate until served.

20 to 30 appetizers.

VARIATION: Wild-rice mixture can be stuffed into sugar-snap or snow-pea pods. Remove strings from pea pods; slit string side of pea pods to open. Fill and refrigerate.

Wild Rice & Lamb Miniature Pastries

½ cup uncooked wild rice (1½ cups cooked)
1 pound ground lamb
1 medium onion, finely chopped
2 cloves garlic, minced
¼ cup olive oil
3 cups diced zucchini
½ cup chicken broth
2 teaspoons dried mint leaves
½ teaspoon grated orange peel
½ teaspoon salt
⅛ teaspoon pepper
Whole-Wheat Pastry (below)

Cook wild rice following one of basic methods (page xvi). Sauté lamb, onion and garlic in olive oil until lamb loses its pink color. Add zucchini and sauté about 5 minutes longer. Add chicken broth, mint, orange peel, salt and pepper; toss to mix thoroughly. Combine with wild rice; cool. Heat oven to 375°F. Roll out pastry; cut into 2-inch rounds with cookie cutter. Place 1 heaping teaspoon of lamb mixture on each round; wet edges lightly with water. Fold in half and press firmly together. Place on cookie sheets. Continue until mixture is used. Bake 12 to 15 minutes.

About 40 (2-inch) pastries.

Whole-Wheat Pastry

1½ cups whole-wheat flour

1½ cups all-purpose flour

1 teaspoon salt

1 cup butter or margarine

9 tablespoons water

Combine flours and salt; cut in butter with pastry blender until mixture is crumbly. Sprinkle on water, 1 tablespoon at a time, mixing with fork until all flour is moistened and dough cleans side of bowl. Shape dough into ball.

Curried Wild Rice Cheese Spheres

⅓ cup uncooked wild rice (1 cup cooked)

1 green onion, sliced

1 teaspoon curry powder

Dash of cayenne pepper

⅓ cup chopped mango chutney, very well drained (optional)

1 (3-ounce) package cream cheese, softened

Chopped pecans or fresh parsley or toasted sesame seeds

Cook wild rice following one of basic methods (page xvi); cool. Blend wild rice, onion, curry powder, cayenne and chutney into cream cheese. Shape into balls the size of small walnuts. Roll in chopped nuts, parsley or sesame seeds or use some of each. Refrigerate until firm.

About 15 appetizers.

Wild Rice Pecan Cheese Ball

8 ounces (about 2 cups) Cheddar cheese,
  shredded
1 (8-ounce) package cream cheese, softened
4 ounces blue cheese, crumbled
½ cup butter or margarine, softened
1 teaspoon Worcestershire sauce
1 teaspoon paprika
¼ teaspoon salt
Pepper to taste
½ cup cooked wild rice
½ cup chopped pecans

Combine cheeses, butter, Worcestershire sauce, paprika, salt and
pepper; shape into a ball. Combine wild rice and pecans; roll ball
in wild rice and pecan mixture; refrigerate. Serve with crackers.

12 to 15 servings.

Popped Wild Rice

Vegetable oil
1 tablespoon uncooked wild rice

Pour vegetable oil into a 6- to 8-inch skillet to the depth of ½ inch. Heat oil almost to the smoking point. Use a small wire strainer in the oil. Place wild rice in the strainer; lower into the hot oil. As soon as the wild rice stops popping, remove the strainer. (Popping only lasts about 2 seconds.) Remove strainer; drain wild rice on paper towels. Repeat. Serve as croutons on soup or salad or sprinkle with salt and serve as a snack.

Apple Wild Rice Breakfast

⅓ cup uncooked wild rice (1 cup cooked)

1 unpeeled apple, cut into ½-inch cubes

1 teaspoon butter

1 to 2 tablespoons brown sugar

¼ teaspoon salt

¼ teaspoon cinnamon

Cook wild rice following one of basic methods (page xvi). Sauté apple in butter in a small skillet over low heat about 5 minutes. Sprinkle brown sugar, salt and cinnamon over apple; stir in wild rice. Heat through. Serve plain or with milk or cream.

2 servings.

VARIATION: Serve cooked wild rice for breakfast; drizzle with honey or maple syrup or sprinkle with brown or granulated sugar; pour on cream.

Soups

Traditionally made of lightweight woods such as cedar, ricing sticks or flails are round and smooth, not over 30 inches long or over 1 pound in weight, and are used in pairs. One stick bends the wild rice grain heads over the edge of the canoe and the other gently taps off ripe rice seeds.

Basic Wild Rice Soup

⅓ cup uncooked wild rice (1 cup cooked)
1½ stalks celery, sliced
1 large onion, sliced
½ pound fresh mushrooms, sliced
½ cup butter or margarine
1 cup all-purpose flour
2 quarts hot chicken broth
Salt and pepper to taste
1 cup half-and-half
2 tablespoons dry white wine

Cook wild rice following one of basic methods (page xvi). Sauté celery, onion and mushrooms in butter; blend in flour. Cook over low heat, stirring until mixture is bubbly. Gradually stir in broth. Heat to boiling, stirring constantly. Boil and stir 1 minute. Stir in salt and pepper and wild rice, then half-and-half and wine. Heat but do not boil.

10 to 12 servings.

Alumni Club Wild Rice Soup

Soup Stock (below)

¼ cup butter or margarine

⅔ cup uncooked wild rice

2 tablespoons sliced blanched almonds

½ cup finely diced onion

½ cup finely diced carrot

¼ cup finely diced celery

2 cups whipping cream

Prepare Soup Stock. Melt butter in heavy kettle; sauté wild rice, almonds, onion, carrot and celery until onion is soft. Add stock; simmer about 1¼ hours. (If necessary, thicken with 2 teaspoons of arrowroot dissolved in a small amount of the cream.) Stir in the cream just before serving.

6 to 8 servings.

Soup Stock

2 duck or chicken carcasses

1 smoked ham bone

1 medium onion, sliced

2 teaspoons Maggi seasoning

Salt and pepper to taste

1 bay leaf

¼ celery stalk, chopped

1¼ quarts water

2 medium carrots, chopped

Combine all ingredients. Heat to boiling; reduce heat and simmer for about 1½ hours. Strain.

Creamy Wild Rice Soup

½ cup uncooked wild rice (1½ cups cooked)
¼ cup chopped onion
6 tablespoons butter or margarine
6 tablespoons all-purpose flour
¼ teaspoon salt
⅛ teaspoon pepper
Dash of allspice
1 (13¾-ounce) can chicken broth
1 cup half-and-half

Cook wild rice following one of basic methods (page xvi). Sauté onion in butter until soft and tender. Stir in flour, salt, pepper and allspice. Cook over low heat, stirring until mixture is bubbly. Gradually add broth. Heat to boiling, stirring constantly. Boil and stir 1 minute. Stir in half-and-half and wild rice; heat through, about 5 to 10 minutes.

4 to 6 servings.

Clear Wild Rice Soup

⅓ cup uncooked wild rice (1 cup cooked)
2 (10¾-ounce) cans chicken broth
1½ cups water
4 green onions, thinly sliced (about ¼ cup)
⅛ teaspoon white pepper
½ cup very thin julienne strips of carrot
½ cup very thin julienne strips of zucchini

Cook wild rice following one of basic methods (page xvi). Simmer chicken broth, water, wild rice, green onions and pepper 10 minutes. Stir in carrot; simmer 5 minutes. Stir in zucchini; simmer 2 minutes longer. Serve immediately.

4 (1-cup) servings.

VARIATION: Substitute sliced fresh mushrooms, julienne strips of cooked chicken or turkey for carrots and zucchini.

Dayton's Special Wild Rice Soup

1²/₃ cups uncooked wild rice (5 cups cooked)
¹/₄ cup minced onion
¹/₃ cup butter or margarine
²/₃ cup all-purpose flour
10²/₃ cups chicken stock or broth
2 cups whipping cream
²/₃ cup dry sherry
Salt and pepper to taste
Parsley, minced

Cook wild rice following one of basic methods (page xvi). Sauté onion in butter until light golden brown. Blend in flour. Cook over low heat, stirring until mixture is bubbly. Gradually stir in stock. Heat to boiling, stirring constantly. Boil and stir 1 minute. Stir in wild rice and simmer 10 minutes. Blend in whipping cream and sherry; simmer until heated through. Correct seasoning if necessary. Garnish with parsley.

4 quarts; 16 (1-cup) servings.

Curried Wild Rice Soup

⅔ cup uncooked wild rice (2 cups cooked)

1 medium onion, chopped

¼ cup butter or margarine

2½ cups sliced fresh mushrooms

½ cup chopped celery

½ cup all-purpose flour

6 cups chicken broth

½ teaspoon salt

½ teaspoon (or more) curry powder

½ teaspoon dry mustard

½ teaspoon paprika

½ teaspoon dried chervil

¼ teaspoon white pepper

2 cups half-and-half

⅔ cup dry sherry

Parsley or chives, chopped

Cook wild rice following one of basic methods (page xvi). Sauté onion in butter in large saucepan until golden brown. Add mushrooms and celery. Cook 2 minutes, stirring constantly. Stir in flour; cook over low heat, stirring until mixture is bubbly. Gradually add broth. Heat to boiling, stirring constantly. Boil and stir 1 minute. Add wild rice, seasonings, half-and-half and sherry; heat to simmer. Ladle into serving bowls. Garnish with parsley.

3 quarts; 12 (1-cup) servings.

Wild Rice & Pecan Soup

1 cup coarsely chopped pecans
½ cup butter or margarine
⅔ cup uncooked wild rice
2 tablespoons chopped green onion
1 clove garlic, minced
8 cups beef broth
2 tablespoons tomato paste
2 tablespoons cornstarch
3 tablespoons water
1 tablespoon dry sherry
1 egg yolk
¼ cup whipping cream
Salt, white pepper and nutmeg to taste

In heavy 4-quart kettle, over medium-to-low heat, sauté pecans in ¼ cup of butter until crispy, about 5 minutes. Remove to bowl and reserve. Rinse wild rice in hot tap water; drain. Heat remaining butter in kettle; add wild rice, onion and garlic; sauté over medium-to-low heat 10 minutes until wild rice is toasted. Add beef broth and tomato paste. Heat to boiling. Reduce heat, cover and simmer 35 to 45 minutes until wild rice is done. Combine cornstarch, water and sherry; stir into boiling mixture. Cook, stirring, until slightly thickened. Blend egg yolk with cream and whisk into the soup. Do not boil after this addition. Taste and add seasoning, if necessary.

6 to 8 servings.

VARIATION: Substitute filberts, toasted almonds, walnuts or peanuts for pecans.

Wild Rice & Chanterelle Soup

¼ cup uncooked wild rice (¾ cup cooked)

1 pound chanterelles (or other fresh mushrooms), cleaned and sliced

2 tablespoons butter or margarine

3 tablespoons all-purpose flour

4 cups beef or chicken stock (preferably homemade)

1 teaspoon paprika

1 teaspoon Dijon-style mustard

2 tablespoons Armagnac or cognac

¼ cup whipping cream

Salt to taste

Partially cook wild rice (about 20 minutes) following one of basic methods (page xvi). Meanwhile, put chanterelles into 3- to 4-quart heavy saucepan with butter and cook over high heat until mushroom juices have begun to evaporate (don't cook until dry); sprinkle with flour. Cook over low heat, stirring until mixture is bubbly. Gradually stir in stock and paprika. Heat to boiling, stirring constantly. Boil and stir 1 minute. Stir in wild rice and cooking liquid; cover and simmer 25 minutes. Whisk in mustard, Armagnac and whipping cream. Correct seasoning if necessary.

4 to 6 servings.

Ham & Wild Rice Soup

¾ cup uncooked wild rice
1 tablespoon vegetable oil
4 cups water
1 medium onion, diced
1 stalk celery, diced
1 carrot, diced
½ cup butter or margarine
½ cup all-purpose flour
3 cups chicken broth
2 cups half-and-half
1 cup diced ham
Salt and pepper to taste
½ teaspoon dried rosemary
Parsley

Rinse and drain wild rice. Sauté in oil until lightly browned; partially cook in water about 30 minutes. Drain, reserving liquid. If necessary, add water to measure 1½ cups. Over medium heat, sauté onion, celery and carrot in butter until onion is transparent; reduce heat. Blend in flour; cook over low heat, stirring until mixture is bubbly. Cook about 5 minutes but do not brown. Using wire whisk, blend in chicken broth and reserved wild-rice water. Heat to boiling, stirring constantly. Boil and stir 1 minute. Add wild rice, half-and-half and ham; blend well. Season with salt and pepper. Stir in rosemary and simmer about 20 minutes; do not boil. Garnish with parsley.

10 (1-cup) servings.

Wild Rice Clam Chowder

½ cup uncooked wild rice (1½ cups cooked)
1 medium onion, diced
¼ green pepper, diced
1 stalk celery, diced
½ cup diced fresh mushrooms
¼ cup butter or margarine
½ cup all-purpose flour
2½ cups homemade chicken stock or canned
    chicken broth
1 pint half-and-half
¼ cup white wine
2 (6½-ounce) cans minced clams
Salt and pepper to taste

Partially cook wild rice (about 20 minutes) following one of basic methods (page xvi). Sauté onion, green pepper, celery and mushrooms in butter until vegetables are soft. Blend in flour, stirring until mixture is bubbly. Gradually stir in chicken stock. Heat to boiling, stirring constantly. Boil and stir 1 minute. Stir in half-and-half and wine. Simmer about 10 minutes. Stir in clams with juice and wild rice. Season with salt and pepper. Simmer about 20 minutes longer.

8 to 10 servings.

Potato Wild Rice Soup

A thick, hearty soup . . .

²/₃ to 1¹/₃ cups uncooked wild rice
Chicken broth
6 to 10 strips bacon
1 small onion, sliced
¹/₂ cup sliced fresh mushrooms
1 quart half-and-half
2 (10³/₄-ounce) cans cream of potato soup
8 ounces (about 2 cups) American, Colby or
   Cheddar cheese, shredded

Partially cook wild rice in chicken broth (about 20 minutes)
following one of basic methods and ratios (page xvi). Fry bacon
until crisp; remove from skillet, drain and crumble. In same
skillet, sauté onion in bacon drippings until onion is transparent;
drain. Combine all ingredients in large kettle; simmer about 30
minutes.

12 servings.

VARIATION: Add 1 (10³/₄-ounce) can cream of chicken soup and
1 (¹/₂-ounce) package Knorr dry mushroom soup mix.

Wild Rice Dumplings

⅓ cup uncooked wild rice (1 cup cooked)

Chicken or beef stock or broth*

1 cup all-purpose flour

2 teaspoons baking powder

½ teaspoon salt

1 egg

½ cup milk

1 tablespoon finely chopped parsley or 1 teaspoon dried parsley flakes

Cook wild rice following one of basic methods (page xvi); cool.
Heat chicken or beef stock in large covered saucepan. Combine
flour, baking powder and salt in bowl. In separate small bowl,
beat egg into milk; stir in parsley. Stir liquid gently into dry
ingredients. Fold in wild rice. Heat spoon by dipping into hot
stock; drop dough by spoonfuls into stock. Dumplings should
barely touch each other. Cover saucepan; simmer 2 minutes.
Turn dumplings; cover and simmer 2 minutes longer. Serve at
once.

12 to 14 dumplings.

*Bouillon cubes dissolved in water can be used for stock.

TIP: A glass cover makes it easy to see when the
dumplings puff up.

Salads

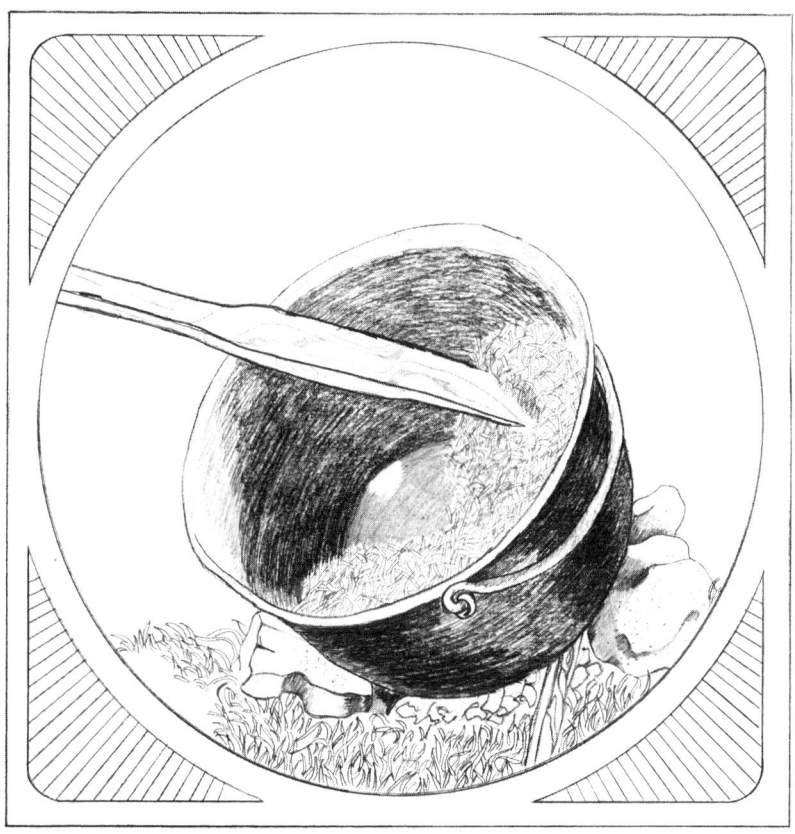

Parching is done to dry the grain so it may be safely stored for use throughout the year. Originally, the grain was sun-dried, but with the coming of the voyageurs and white settlers, metal pots became available and were soon adopted. Green rice, stirred with a paddle, is parched in caldrons over open fires.

Mahnomen Waldorf Salad

⅔ cup uncooked wild rice (2 cups cooked)

2 large apples

1 tablespoon lemon juice

2 tablespoons brown sugar

2 stalks celery, sliced

⅓ cup mayonnaise

½ cup dairy sour cream

Cook wild rice following one of basic methods (page xvi); chill. Dice unpeeled apples and toss with mixture of lemon juice and brown sugar. Stir in celery and wild rice. Blend mayonnaise with sour cream and toss with salad ingredients, mixing well. Refrigerate until thoroughly chilled, but not longer than 6 to 8 hours. Serve on lettuce leaves, if desired.

6 servings.

Wild Rice Fruit Salad

1 cup uncooked wild rice (3 cups cooked)

1 (20-ounce) can pineapple chunks, drained

1 (11-ounce) can mandarin oranges, drained

1 (3-ounce) jar maraschino cherries, drained and halved

1 cup chopped walnuts

1 cup miniature marshmallows

1 (3-ounce) package orange-flavored gelatin (not dissolved)

1 (9-ounce) carton frozen whipped topping, thawed

Shredded coconut

Cook wild rice following one of basic methods (page xvi); chill. Combine all ingredients except coconut in large bowl. Sprinkle with coconut. Keeps well, refrigerated.

8 to 10 servings.

Spinach Wild Rice Salad

1 cup uncooked wild rice (3 cups cooked)
1/4 cup vegetable oil
2 tablespoons white wine vinegar
2 teaspoons soy sauce
1 teaspoon sugar
1/4 teaspoon ground ginger
2 cups finely torn fresh spinach
1 to 2 tomatoes, chopped
1 cup sliced cauliflowerets
1/2 cup sliced green onions
1/2 cup crisply fried crumbled bacon

Cook wild rice following one of basic methods (page xvi); cool slightly. Combine oil, vinegar, soy sauce, sugar and ginger. Add to warm rice. Cover and refrigerate. Before serving, fold in remaining ingredients.

8 to 10 servings.

Wild Rice & Green Bean Salad

²/₃ cup uncooked wild rice (2 cups cooked)

1 pound tender, fresh green beans, trimmed

1 (3-inch) piece fresh ginger root, peeled

3 tablespoons wine vinegar or sherry

1 teaspoon sesame oil

¹/₂ teaspoon coarse salt

¹/₂ teaspoon sugar

¹/₈ teaspoon freshly ground white pepper

¹/₃ cup olive or vegetable oil

¹/₄ cup sesame seeds, toasted

Cook wild rice following one of basic methods (page xvi); cool. Cut beans on diagonal, into ¹/₄-inch lengths. Drop into rapidly boiling water; cook until just tender-crisp, about 3 minutes. Drain thoroughly and rinse immediately under cold running water. Combine beans with wild rice. Put ginger root and vinegar into food processor or blender. Process until ginger is puréed; drain liquid and discard pulp. Put vinegar, sesame oil, coarse salt, sugar and pepper into small bowl. Whisk in oil until mixture is emulsified. Add beans and rice. Toss to coat with dressing. Cover; refrigerate 4 hours. Arrange salad in serving bowl and top with sesame seeds.

6 servings.

Festive Wild Rice Salad

The red and green peppers make this an attractive holiday salad.

1 cup uncooked wild rice (3 cups cooked)

1 cup chopped fresh mushrooms

1/2 cup chopped celery

1/2 cup chopped green pepper

1/2 cup chopped red (sweet) pepper

1/4 cup chopped onion

1/4 cup sliced ripe olives

1/4 cup sliced stuffed olives

3 hard-cooked eggs, chopped

1 cup mayonnaise or salad dressing

1/4 cup sugar

2 tablespoons cider vinegar

1 1/2 teaspoons prepared mustard

1/4 teaspoon dry mustard

Cook wild rice following one of basic methods (page xvi); chill. Combine rice with vegetables, olives and eggs. Combine remaining ingredients; stir into rice mixture. Refrigerate until served.

12 servings.

Wild Rice Tarragon Salad

1 cup uncooked wild rice (3 cups cooked)
3 cups chicken broth
1 (9- to 10-ounce) package frozen Italian
    green beans
1 cup carrot slices
½ cup diced green pepper
½ cup diced celery
6 green onions, chopped
Tarragon Dressing (below)

Cook wild rice in chicken broth following one of basic methods
(page xvi); cool. Rinse frozen beans with hot tap water to thaw;
drain. Combine wild rice with vegetables; pour Tarragon Dressing over all. Refrigerate several hours.

6 to 8 servings.

Tarragon Dressing

⅓ cup tarragon vinegar
¼ cup vegetable oil
1½ teaspoons salt
1 teaspoon sugar
1 teaspoon dried tarragon
Pepper, freshly ground, to taste

Combine all ingredients in small saucepan; heat to boiling. Boil
gently 3 minutes; cool.

Summer Days Wild Rice Salad

⅔ cup uncooked wild rice (2 cups cooked)
½ cup thinly sliced green onion
½ cup chopped parsley
⅓ cup chopped fresh mint leaves
⅔ cup olive oil
⅓ cup lemon juice
⅛ teaspoon freshly ground pepper
Fresh inner romaine lettuce leaves
1 medium tomato, seeded and chopped
Alfalfa sprouts

Cook wild rice following one of basic methods (page xvi); cool. Mix wild rice with green onion, parsley, mint leaves, olive oil, lemon juice and pepper. Cover and refrigerate at least 2 hours for flavors to blend. Serve over a bed of romaine; garnish with tomato and alfalfa sprouts. Can also be served as pita (pocket) bread sandwich filling, with shredded cheese and additional fresh vegetables.

6 servings.

Curried Wild Rice Salad

¾ cup uncooked wild rice (2¼ cups cooked)

1 (4-ounce) jar marinated artichoke hearts
  packed in oil, drained and quartered

12 stuffed green olives, sliced

4 green onions, sliced

½ cup mayonnaise or salad dressing

1½ teaspoons curry powder

¼ cup chopped parsley

Cook wild rice following one of basic methods (page xvi); cool. In mixing bowl, combine wild rice, artichoke hearts, olives and onions. In small bowl, combine mayonnaise and curry powder; gently stir into wild rice mixture. Serve immediately or cover and refrigerate until serving time. Garnish with parsley just before serving.

6 servings.

Marinated Wild Rice Salad

2 cups uncooked wild rice
⅓ cup olive oil
4 cups chicken broth
⅓ to ½ cup Vinaigrette Dressing (page 37)
⅔ cup sliced water chestnuts
½ cup sliced red pepper
¼ cup sliced green onions
Salt and pepper to taste
12 ounces snow peas
8 ounces fresh mushrooms, sliced

Sauté wild rice in olive oil; cook 5 minutes or until lightly browned. Combine with chicken broth in casserole; bake at 325°F for 1½ hours. (If wild rice seems too moist, remove cover and bake an additional 5 to 10 minutes.) Prepare Vinaigrette Dressing. Transfer wild rice to bowl and toss with ⅓ to ½ cup of dressing. Combine with water chestnuts, red pepper, green onions, salt and pepper. Refrigerate several hours or overnight. String pea pods and blanch in boiling salted water 30 seconds. Refresh under cold water and pat dry. Cut pea pods diagonally into 1-inch lengths and reserve. Marinate mushrooms in dressing; reserve. Marinate snow peas in dressing only about 1 hour before serving. (If marinated too. long, color will fade.) To serve, place rice mixture in serving bowl, make a well in center and mound peas and mushrooms in well.

6 to 8 servings.

Vinaigrette Dressing

⅓ cup wine vinegar

2 teaspoons Dijon-style mustard

1 teaspoon salt

Pepper to taste

2 sprigs parsley (optional)

1 cup vegetable oil, part olive (optional)

Place vinegar, mustard, salt, pepper and parsley in food processor or blender; blend. Gradually add oil until thoroughly blended.

VARIATIONS: Place vinegar, mustard, salt, pepper and finely chopped parsley in mixing bowl; gradually add oil and beat with a whisk until blended.

Makes 2⅓ cups.

Wild Rice Salad with Basil

½ cup uncooked wild rice (1½ cups cooked)

2 tomatoes, chopped

3 green onions, including tops, finely
    chopped

3 tablespoons chopped fresh basil

2 teaspoons olive oil

¾ teaspoon garlic salt, or to taste

Lettuce

Cook wild rice following one of basic methods (page xvi); chill. Combine with tomatoes, green onions, basil, olive oil and garlic salt, tossing lightly. Serve on bed of lettuce.

4 servings.

Wild Rice Tabbouli

2⅓ cups uncooked wild rice (7 cups cooked)

¾ cup chopped green pepper

½ cup chopped green onions, including tops

¾ to 1 cup chopped fresh mint

½ to ¾ cup chopped parsley

⅓ cup lemon juice

⅓ cup olive oil

½ teaspoon salt

½ teaspoon pepper

Cook wild rice following one of basic methods (page xvi); cool. Combine all ingredients and refrigerate several hours or overnight. Can also be served as pita (pocket) bread sandwich filling.

16 to 20 servings.

VARIATION: 6 medium tomatoes, chopped, can be added or used as decoration around serving bowl.

Byerly's Wild Rice Salad

1½ cups uncooked wild rice (4½ cups
   cooked
¾ cup thinly sliced green onion
¾ cup diced celery
½ cup slivered almonds, toasted
3 tablespoons olive oil
3 tablespoons safflower oil
3 tablespoons white wine vinegar
¾ teaspoon dried thyme, crushed
½ teaspoon salt
¼ teaspoon pepper

Cook wild rice following one of basic methods (page xvi); cool.
Combine green onion, celery and almonds with wild rice in large
bowl. In small bowl, whisk oils into vinegar 1 drop at a time; stir
in thyme, salt and pepper. Pour over rice mixture; toss lightly.
Serve chilled.

12 (½-cup) servings.

VARIATION: Add ½ cup chopped green pepper, 1 (4-ounce) jar
chopped pimento, drained, and 1 (8-ounce) can shoe-peg corn,
drained, to rice mixture.

Wild Rice & Artichoke Heart Salad

1 cup uncooked wild rice (3 cups cooked)

2 (7¼-ounce) jars marinated artichoke hearts, packed in oil

3 tomatoes, diced

1 (8-ounce) can sliced water chestnuts, drained

1 (4-ounce) can mushrooms, drained

1 cup bottled Italian dressing

Cook wild rice following one of basic methods (page xvi); cool. Drain 1 jar of artichoke hearts. Combine wild rice, artichoke hearts including juice from 1 jar, tomatoes, water chestnuts and mushrooms. Pour dressing over mixture. Marinate overnight in refrigerator. Drain before serving. Serve chilled.

8 to 10 servings.

Gitchi' Gumi' Salad

1⅓ cups uncooked wild rice (4 cups cooked)

1 (8-ounce) package wild and long grain rice
   mix

½ cup bottled French dressing

½ cup diced celery

½ cup chopped green pepper

½ cup diced green onions

½ cup sliced fresh mushrooms

¼ cup chopped parsley

1 pound cooked shrimp

Cook wild rice following one of basic methods (page xvi); cool.
Cook rice mix following package directions; cool. Combine wild
rice and rice mix; add French dressing and vegetables. Mix well.
Pack tightly in lightly oiled 6-cup ring mold; chill. Unmold on
salad greens. Put shrimp in center and serve with additional French
dressing.

6 to 8 servings.

Wild Rice, Fruit & Shrimp Salad

⅔ cup uncooked wild rice (2 cups cooked)

2 cups whole seedless green grapes

2 cups cooked or canned medium shrimp, drained

2 cups chopped celery

1 cup coarsely chopped walnuts

½ cup mayonnaise

½ cup dairy sour cream

2 tablespoons bacon bits

Pimento

Ripe olives

Cook wild rice following one of basic methods (page xvi); chill. Combine with grapes, shrimp, celery and walnuts. Combine mayonnaise, sour cream and bacon bits; stir into wild rice mixture. Garnish with pimento and ripe olives. Refrigerate before serving.

10 to 12 servings.

Wild Rice Seafood Salad

*For a more lavish salad, use fresh or frozen
crab, lobster, shrimp or scallops; however,
you'll be surprised how well tuna blends with
the flavor of the wild rice!*

⅔ cup uncooked wild rice (2 cups cooked)

⅓ cup mayonnaise

⅓ cup dairy sour cream

¼ cup tomato-based chili sauce

1 tablespoon lemon juice

1 teaspoon Dijon-style mustard

1 large tomato, peeled, seeded and diced

1 cup thinly sliced celery

½ cup thinly sliced green onions

½ pound fresh crab, cooked and chilled, or
1 (7-ounce) package frozen crabmeat,
thawed and drained or 1 (7-ounce) can
water-packed tuna, drained

Salt and pepper to taste

Lettuce

Parsley, chopped, or hard-cooked eggs,
sliced

Cook wild rice following one of basic methods (page xvi); cool.
Blend mayonnaise, sour cream, chili sauce, lemon juice and mustard in large bowl. Gently fold in wild rice, tomato, celery, onions
and seafood until blended. Season with salt and pepper. Serve
in individual lettuce cups; garnish with parsley and/or egg slices.

4 to 6 servings.

Polynesian Salad

1²/₃ cups uncooked wild rice (5 cups cooked)

4 to 5 cups cubed cooked turkey

1 (20-ounce) can pineapple chunks, drained and halved

2 cups halved seedless green grapes

2 (8-ounce) cans sliced water chestnuts, drained

1½ cups mayonnaise

⅓ cup chopped chutney

¾ teaspoon seasoned salt

1 cup salted cashew nut pieces

Lettuce leaves

Cook wild rice following one of basic methods (page xvi); cool. Combine wild rice with turkey, pineapple, grapes and water chestnuts. Combine mayonnaise, chutney and salt. Gently combine with salad ingredients. Cover and refrigerate. Just before serving, stir in cashews, saving some for garnish. Serve in lettuce-lined bowl.

12 servings.

Chicken Wild Rice Salad

1 cup uncooked wild rice (3 cups cooked)

1 heaping tablespoon instant chicken bouillon (or 3 chicken bouillon cubes)

3 cooked chicken breasts, cubed

1 cup finely chopped celery

2 bunches green onions, including tops,
finely sliced

1 green pepper, finely chopped

1 (4-ounce) can mushrooms, drained and
chopped

1 to 1½ cups salad dressing or mayonnaise

1 (8-ounce) can water chestnuts, drained and
diced

1 (2-ounce) jar chopped pimento, drained

1 hard-cooked egg, finely chopped

Cook wild rice with bouillon, following one of basic methods
(page xvi); cool. Combine wild rice, chicken, celery, green onions, green pepper and mushrooms. Refrigerate several hours or
overnight to blend flavors. Just before serving, gently stir in salad
dressing, water chestnuts and pimento. Garnish with egg.

6 to 8 servings.

Wild Rice Chicken Salad with Red Pepper Vinaigrette

A favorite for a hot summer day or a make-ahead luncheon.

1½ cups uncooked wild rice (4½ cups cooked)

Red Pepper Vinaigrette (page 47)

2 cups cubed cooked chicken

1 cup diced celery

½ cup chopped parsley

½ cup sliced green onion, including tops

2 tablespoons chopped fresh (or 2 teaspoons dried) tarragon

Butter lettuce or other lettuce

Tomato wedges

½ cup toasted slivered almonds, pistachios or pine nuts

Cook wild rice following one of basic methods (page xvi); cool. While rice is cooking, prepare Red Pepper Vinaigrette. Combine wild rice, chicken, celery, parsley, green onion and tarragon in large bowl. Mix in vinaigrette. Line serving bowl or platter with lettuce. Turn mixture into serving dish; garnish with tomato wedges and sprinkle with nuts.

6 to 8 servings.

Red Pepper Vinaigrette

3 tablespoons white wine vinegar
2 tablespoons Dijon-style mustard
1 teaspoon salt
$\frac{1}{2}$ teaspoon freshly ground black pepper
$\frac{1}{8}$ to $\frac{1}{4}$ teaspoon crushed red pepper flakes
$\frac{3}{4}$ cup olive or safflower oil

Place vinegar, mustard, salt, black and red pepper in bowl. Whisk in oil to make a smooth thickened dressing.

Wild Rice, Chicken & Pasta Salad

²/₃ cup uncooked wild rice (2 cups cooked)

¹/₃ cup pine nuts or slivered almonds

1 teaspoon butter or margarine

6 chicken breast halves, skinned and boned (about 1¹/₂ pounds)

¹/₂ cup chicken stock

1 pound linguine, cooked *al dente* and drained

1 (15-ounce) can garbanzo beans, drained

2 (6-ounce) jars marinated artichoke hearts, drained

1 (10-ounce) package frozen peas

8 ounces fresh mushrooms, sliced

1 red or green bell pepper, seeded and cut into thin strips

1 (2-ounce) jar pimento-stuffed green olives, drained and sliced

1 (2-ounce) can sliced ripe olives, drained.

Dressing (page 49)

Cook wild rice following one of the basic methods (page xvi); cool. Toast nuts in butter in small skillet; set aside. In another shallow pan, put chicken breasts skinned-side up and add chicken stock. Cover; simmer 25 minutes until chicken is cooked white all the way through. Cool in stock. Drain; cut into strips. Combine with remaining ingredients. Pour Dressing over salad and toss well. Can be made a day in advance; keep refrigerated.

8 to 10 servings.

Dressing

½ cup olive oil

2 to 3 tablespoons red wine vinegar

¼ cup minced fresh parsley

2 teaspoons Dijon-style mustard

½ teaspoon curry powder

Salt and freshly ground pepper, to taste

Whisk all ingredients together until well blended.

Wild Rice Arabian Nights Salad

⅔ cup uncooked wild rice (2 cups cooked)

2 cups finely diced cooked chicken

½ cup olive or vegetable oil

¼ cup lemon juice

1 cup chopped parsley

½ cup chopped green onion

3 tablespoons chopped fresh (or 1 tablespoon dried) mint leaves

½ pint cherry tomatoes, quartered

Cook wild rice following one of basic methods (page xvi); cool.
In large bowl, combine with chicken, oil, lemon juice, parsley,
onion and mint; cover and refrigerate until thoroughly chilled.
Just before serving, add tomatoes and toss gently. Garnish with
lemon wedges, if desired.

4 servings.

Wild Rice Turkey Salad

If you don't have any leftover roast turkey, get some at the deli.

⅔ cup uncooked wild rice (2 cups cooked)

⅔ cup mayonnaise

⅓ cup milk

2 tablespoons lemon juice

½ small onion, grated or minced

3 cups cubed cooked turkey

1 (8-ounce) can sliced water chestnuts, drained

½ pound seedless green grapes, halved (about 2 cups)

1 cup cashew nuts

Salt and pepper to taste

Lemon slices (optional)

Cook wild rice following one of basic methods (page xvi); cool. In large bowl, combine mayonnaise, milk, lemon juice and onion until well mixed. Stir in rice, turkey and water chestnuts; refrigerate until thoroughly chilled. Just before serving, fold in grapes and nuts. Season with salt and pepper. Spoon onto platter lined with lettuce leaves; garnish with lemon slices.

6 servings.

Wild Rice Salad Andalouse

²/₃ cup uncooked wild rice (2 cups cooked)

1 cup diced turkey ham or regular ham

²/₃ cup fresh or frozen peas, cooked

1 (6-ounce) can marinated artichoke hearts, drained

4 ounces fresh mushrooms, sliced

¹/₃ cup golden raisins

1 tablespoon minced chives

Bibb or garden lettuce or watercress

Fresh parsley

Oil and vinegar dressing

Cook wild rice following one of basic methods (page xvi); chill. Combine wild rice with ham, peas, artichoke hearts, mushrooms, raisins and chives; toss to blend. Refrigerate 1 to 2 hours; toss again. Arrange on crisp lettuce; garnish with parsley. Serve with favorite oil and vinegar dressing.

4 to 6 servings.

Ham & Wild Rice Salad

1 to 1⅓ cups uncooked wild rice (3 or 4
  cups cooked)

1 pound ham, cubed (about 3 cups)

2 medium avocados, peeled and cut into
  bite-size pieces

1 tablespoon lemon juice

2 tomatoes, cubed and seeded

1 cup chopped celery

¾ cup finely sliced green onion, including
  tops

¼ cup finely chopped parsley

2 tablespoons chopped pimento

½ cup vegetable oil

¼ cup red wine vinegar

Salt and freshly ground pepper, to taste

Cook wild rice following one of basic methods (page xvi); cool.
Place wild rice and ham in bowl. Sprinkle avocado with lemon
juice; add to rice and ham. Add tomatoes, celery, onion, parsley,
pimento, oil, vinegar, salt and pepper. Toss to blend; refrigerate
until served.

8 servings.

VARIATION: Substitute smoked turkey for ham.

Entrées & Stuffings

To thresh, parched wild rice was placed in a shallow hole in the ground lined with deer skins. Wearing special soft moccasins and leather leggings called gaiters, the Indians danced or "jigged" on the wild rice to loosen the tough outer hulls.

55

Calico Wild Rice

½ cup uncooked wild rice (1½ cups cooked)
3 carrots, cut into ¼-inch slices
¾ pound chuck or round steak, partially frozen
Butter or margarine
1 clove garlic, split
1 (10-ounce) package frozen cut green beans
1 small onion, thinly sliced
½ teaspoon salt

Cook wild rice following one of basic methods (page xvi). In small amount of lightly salted water, cook carrots, covered, 5 minutes. Drain and set aside. Slice steak very thinly, on diagonal. In large skillet, heat 2 tablespoons butter with garlic. Add steak slices; cook quickly until well browned on both sides. Remove and set aside. To the drippings, add carrots, green beans and onion. Cook, covered, until tender, about 5 minutes. Add more butter if needed, stirring once or twice. Discard garlic. Add meat and wild rice to skillet of vegetables. Add salt and a little more butter if it seems dry. Toss vegetables, wild rice and meat mixture together. Heat thoroughly. Serve immediately.

4 servings.

Oven Beef Stroganoff

½ cup butter

1½ pounds beef, cut into thin strips

8 ounces fresh mushrooms, thinly sliced

1 large onion, chopped

2 tablespoons tomato paste

1 tablespoon paprika

2 cups dairy sour cream

1½ cups uncooked wild rice (4 cups cooked)

1 tablespoon lemon juice

1 teaspoon salt

¼ teaspoon pepper

Divide butter into three portions. Heat one portion in skillet; add half the meat and brown. Put into shallow 11¾ × 7½-inch baking dish. Repeat with second portion of butter and remaining meat. Add third portion of butter; brown mushrooms and onion. Stir in tomato paste and paprika. Remove from heat and stir in sour cream. Pour over meat in casserole; cover. Bake at 350°F for 30 to 40 minutes. In the meantime, cook wild rice following one of basic methods (page xvi). Just before serving, stir lemon juice, salt and pepper into the stroganoff. Serve on bed of hot cooked wild rice.

4 to 6 servings.

TIP: Serve any of the following on a bed of hot cooked wild rice (they can make an ordinary meal special—and a special one even more so!):
Beef Burgundy; Chicken or Lamb Curry; Shish Kabobs; Swedish Meatballs; Fish or Beef Stew.

Meaty Wild Rice Casserole

¾ cup uncooked wild rice (2¼ cups cooked)
½ cup uncooked white rice
1 cup chopped onion
½ pound lean beef, cut into ½-inch cubes
½ pound lean pork, cut into ½-inch cubes
2 tablespoons shortening
2 to 4 tablespoons soy sauce
1 (10¾-ounce) can cream of mushroom soup
½ cup water
1¾ to 2 cups chopped celery

Cook wild rice following one of basic methods (page xvi). In separate saucepan, cook white rice following package directions. Sauté onion, beef and pork in shortening. Combine with cooked rices, soy sauce, mushroom soup, water and celery. Pour into greased 2-quart casserole; cover. Bake at 375°F for 50 to 60 minutes.

6 servings.

VARIATION: All beef can be substituted for pork and beef; add mushrooms and/or 1 green pepper, chopped, if desired.

TIP: Greasing or spraying a casserole with nonstick coating makes cleanup after cooking easier and faster.

Wild Rice Plus

2 cups chopped celery
1½ large onions, chopped
1 clove garlic, minced (optional)
½ to ¾ pound lean pork, cubed
½ to ¾ pound veal or beef, cubed
2 tablespoons butter
½ cup uncooked wild rice
½ cup uncooked white rice
4 cups boiling water
¼ cup soy sauce
1 teaspoon salt

Brown celery, onions, garlic and meat in butter. Combine with remaining ingredients in large greased casserole; mix thoroughly. Bake at 350°F for 1 to 1½ hours. Serve with mushroom sauce, if desired.

6 to 8 servings.

VARIATIONS: Substitute consommé for boiling water; add 8 ounces fresh mushrooms, sliced, 1 (8-ounce) can sliced water chestnuts, drained, with other ingredients. Sprinkle top with ½ cup slivered almonds during last 5 minutes of baking.

Rosy Wild Rice Casserole

1 cup uncooked wild rice

2 pounds ground beef

1 medium onion, chopped

1 (10¾-ounce) can tomato soup

1 (10¾-ounce) can cream of mushroom soup

½ cup catsup

½ cup dry bread crumbs

1 tablespoon sugar

Salt and pepper to taste

Pour boiling water to cover over wild rice and let stand overnight; drain. Cook and stir ground beef and onion until ground beef is brown; drain if necessary. Add soups, catsup, bread crumbs, sugar, salt and pepper. Pour into greased 2-quart casserole. Bake at 350°F for 1½ hours.

8 to 10 servings.

Many recipes for casseroles similar to those that follow were received from contributors. Any of them can be varied by adding more or less mushrooms, celery, onion or green pepper. And any of the cream soups, mushroom, celery or chicken can be interchanged, according to personal preference.

Wild Rice Baron

2 cups uncooked wild rice (6 cups cooked)

2 pounds lean ground beef

1 pound fresh mushrooms

½ cup chopped celery

1 cup chopped onion

½ cup butter

2 cups dairy sour cream

¼ cup soy sauce

2 teaspoons salt

¼ teaspoon pepper

½ cup slivered almonds

Cook wild rice following one of basic methods (page xvi). Brown ground beef; set aside. Clean mushrooms; slice. Sauté mushrooms, celery and onion in butter 5 to 10 minutes. Combine sour cream, soy sauce, salt and pepper. Add wild rice, ground beef, sautéed vegetables and almonds (reserving a few for garnish). Toss lightly. Place mixture in a lightly greased 3-quart casserole. Bake at 350°F for about 1 hour. Stir several times during baking. Add more water, if needed, and season to taste. Garnish with reserved almonds and sprigs of parsley, or sour cream laced with soy sauce, if desired.

10 to 12 servings.

Stuffed Peppers

½ to ⅔ cup uncooked wild rice (about 1¾ cups cooked)

½ pound ground beef

1 medium onion, chopped

1 teaspoon salt

1 carrot, diced

½ cup chopped celery

6 medium green peppers

Cheddar cheese, shredded

Cook wild rice following one of basic methods (page xvi). Brown ground beef and onion in skillet; drain well. Season with salt. Add carrot and celery. Simmer 20 minutes. Meanwhile, cut a thin slice from stem end of each pepper. Remove membrane and seeds; rinse. Cook peppers 3 minutes in enough boiling water to cover; drain. Stuff peppers with wild rice mixture; top with cheese. Stand upright in baking dish. Bake at 375°F for 35 minutes.

6 servings.

Oriental Wild Rice Casserole

2 cups uncooked wild rice
1 cup chopped celery
1/2 cup chopped onion
1/2 green pepper, chopped
2 tablespoons butter or margarine
1 1/2 pounds ground beef
1 (4-ounce) can mushrooms
2 (10 3/4-ounce) cans cream of mushroom
   soup
1 1/2 cups beef broth
3 tablespoons soy sauce
Salt and pepper to taste
Slivered almonds

Partially cook wild rice (about 10 minutes) following one of basic methods (page xvi); drain. Sauté celery, onion and green pepper in butter until tender but not brown. Remove from pan; crumble and brown ground beef in same skillet. Add mushrooms, soup, broth, soy sauce, vegetables and wild rice; mix well. Season to taste. Place in casserole and sprinkle with almonds. Bake at 300° to 325°F for 1 1/2 to 2 hours. Add more broth if casserole seems dry.

6 servings.

VARIATION: Add 1 (8-ounce) can sliced water chestnuts, drained, 1 (8-ounce) can bamboo shoots, drained, and 1 cup dairy sour cream.

Hunter's Meat Loaf

½ cup uncooked wild rice

1 cup water

1 pound ground venison

½ pound ground beef

2 eggs, beaten

¼ cup chopped onion

2 tablespoons catsup

1 cup milk

1½ teaspoons salt

¼ teaspoon pepper

Rinse and drain wild rice. Cook wild rice in water 15 minutes; drain. Combine wild rice with remaining ingredients; shape into loaf. Put into 9 × 5 × 3-inch pan. Bake at 350°F for 1 hour. Place on serving plate; garnish with catsup or barbecue sauce and parsley, if desired.

6 servings.

VARIATION: Use all ground beef instead of venison and beef.

TIP: Most casseroles can be prepared ahead and refrigerated until time to bake. Allow a few more minutes baking time.

Wild Rice Company Casserole

2 cups boiling water
²⁄₃ cup uncooked wild rice
1 (10½-ounce) can chicken with rice soup
1 (4-ounce) can mushrooms
½ cup water
1 bay leaf
1 teaspoon salt
¼ teaspoon celery salt
¼ teaspoon garlic salt
¼ teaspoon onion salt
¼ teaspoon paprika
¼ teaspoon pepper
3 tablespoons chopped onion
3 tablespoons vegetable oil
¾ pound lean ground beef

Pour boiling water over wild rice. Let stand, covered, 15 minutes; drain. Place wild rice in greased 2-quart casserole. Add soup, mushrooms and liquid, water and seasonings. Mix gently and let stand for a few minutes. Sauté onion in oil until transparent. Remove and add to casserole. Brown beef in same skillet and gently stir into rice; cover. Bake at 325°F for 2 hours. Remove bay leaf before serving.

4 servings.

Savory Casserole

1 cup uncooked wild rice

4 cups boiling water

1 (10¾-ounce) can cream of mushroom soup

1 (10¾-ounce) can cream of chicken soup

1 (8-ounce) can mushrooms

2 beef bouillon cubes or 2 teaspoons instant beef bouillon

1 cup boiling water

1 bay leaf

¼ teaspoon celery salt

¼ teaspoon pepper

¼ teaspoon onion salt

¼ teaspoon paprika

¾ cup chopped celery

6 tablespoons chopped onion

¼ cup butter or margarine

1½ pounds ground beef

½ cup slivered almonds

Pour 4 cups boiling water over wild rice. Let stand 15 minutes; drain. Stir in soups, mushrooms with liquid, bouillon cubes, 1 cup water, bay leaf and seasonings. Sauté celery and onion in butter until transparent; add to rice mixture. Brown ground beef; drain and add to wild rice mixture. Pour into large casserole and sprinkle with almonds. Bake, covered, at 350°F for 1½ hours. Add more water if necessary. May be made ahead and refrigerated until time to bake. Remove bay leaf before serving.

10 servings.

VARIATION: Soak wild rice overnight in water to cover. Fry 4 to 6 strips cut-up bacon in large skillet; drain. Add bacon and ¼ cup chopped green pepper with the ground beef, celery and onions.

Wild Rice & Peas

½ cup uncooked wild rice

1 pound ground beef

1 medium onion, finely chopped

½ cup sliced celery

3 tablespoons soy sauce

1 (10¾-ounce) can cream of mushroom soup

1 (10¾-ounce) can cream of chicken soup

1½ cups water

1 (10-ounce) package frozen peas, thawed

Chow mein noodles

Rinse and drain wild rice. Brown ground beef with onion; drain if necessary. Add wild rice and remaining ingredients except chow mein noodles. Pour into lightly greased casserole. Bake at 350°F for 45 minutes. Top with chow mein noodles and bake 15 minutes longer.

6 servings.

Wild Rice & Bean Sprouts

1 cup uncooked wild rice (3 cups cooked)

1 pound coarsely ground pork or veal

2 cups sliced celery

1 small green pepper, chopped

1 onion, chopped

1 carrot, shredded

1 (4-ounce) can mushrooms

1 (16-ounce) can bean sprouts, drained

1 (10¾-ounce) can cream of mushroom soup

1 tablespoon soy sauce

1 tablespoon Worcestershire sauce

Salt and pepper to taste

Cook wild rice following one of basic methods (page xvi). Brown meat in skillet until no longer pink; add remaining ingredients. Mix gently and pour into greased 3-quart casserole; cover. Bake at 375°F for 1 hour. Add water during baking, if necessary.

6 servings.

Winter Sausage Bake

1 pound bulk pork sausage

1 pound small fresh mushrooms

2 medium onions, chopped

2 cups uncooked wild rice

1 cup water

1/4 cup all-purpose flour

1/2 cup whipping cream

2 1/2 cups condensed chicken broth

1 tablespoon salt

Dash of pepper

Dash of Tabasco sauce

1/8 teaspoon dried oregano

1/8 teaspoon dried marjoram

1/8 teaspoon dried thyme

1/2 cup slivered almonds, toasted

Crumble and fry sausage. Remove from skillet and drain. Clean mushrooms; sauté mushrooms and onions in small amount of sausage drippings. Reserve a few mushroom caps for topping. Rinse and drain wild rice; cook in water about 10 minutes. Mix flour with whipping cream; add chicken broth. Season with salt and pepper, Tabasco and herbs. Mix sausage, onions, mushrooms, wild rice and broth mixture. Pour into greased 3-quart casserole. Bake at 350°F for 45 minutes. Remove from oven; sprinkle top with slivered almonds and reserved mushroom caps.

10 to 12 servings.

The Governor's Sarma

1 cup uncooked wild rice (3 cups cooked)

1 large head cabbage

Boiling water

1 to 2 tablespoons vinegar

2 quarts sauerkraut

1 large onion, chopped

2 tablespoons vegetable oil

1½ pounds ground pork

1 pound ground ham

½ pound ground beef

½ tablespoon minced garlic

1 egg

Salt and pepper to taste

1 (10¾-ounce) can tomato soup

½ pound bacon

3 cups cold water

Cook wild rice following one of basic methods (page xvi). To sour cabbage, place in boiling water to cover for 10 to 15 minutes, or until leaves soften. Add vinegar to help sour cabbage. (Another way is to freeze cabbage head in advance and thaw.) Rinse each leaf; drain in colander. Rinse and drain sauerkraut. Brown onion in oil; mix with meats, garlic, wild rice, egg, salt and pepper. Roll a generous portion of meat mixture in each cabbage leaf. When leaves are used, shape remaining meat into balls. Cover bottom of large roasting pan with sauerkraut and place rolls on top. Place meatballs between cabbage rolls. If more than one layer of rolls is necessary, place a layer of sauerkraut between. End with a layer of sauerkraut; spoon tomato soup over sauerkraut. Place bacon

slices over tomato soup. Add cold water; cover. Bake at 350°F for 2 to 2½ hours, adding more water if necessary.

About 22 sarmas.

VARIATION: Sarmas can be made smaller and served as appetizers.

ℋam & Cheese Wild Rice

1 cup uncooked wild rice (3 cups cooked)

2½ cups cut broccoli

2 cups cubed cooked ham

4 ounces (about 1 cup) Cheddar cheese, shredded

1 (10¾-ounce) can cream of celery soup

1 cup mayonnaise

2 teaspoons dry mustard

½ cup grated Parmesan cheese

Cook wild rice following one of basic methods (page xvi). Grease a flat 2-quart casserole. Place wild rice in casserole. Cook broccoli just until tender-crisp; drain and spread over rice. Add ham; top with Cheddar cheese. Combine soup, mayonnaise and mustard; spread over cheese. Sprinkle with Parmesan cheese; cover with foil. Bake at 350°F for 45 minutes.

6 servings.

Creamy Wild Rice & Ham Rolls

⅔ cup uncooked wild rice (2 cups cooked)

¼ pound fresh mushrooms

⅓ cup butter or margarine

1 medium onion, chopped

¼ cup all-purpose flour

1 cup chicken or beef broth

1 cup half-and-half

Salt and pepper to taste

8 large (⅛-inch thick) slices boiled ham, roast beef or turkey breast (about ¾ pound)

Cook wild rice following one of basic methods (page xvi). Meanwhile, flute the caps of four of the largest mushrooms; remove stems. Slice stems and remaining mushrooms. Heat oven to 350°F. In a medium saucepan, cook mushroom caps in butter until golden; remove to drain on paper towels. Add sliced mushrooms and onion; cook just until onion is tender. Stir in flour; remove from heat. Gradually stir in broth until blended. Return to heat; cook

and stir until mixture boils; boil and stir 1 minute. Stir in half-and-half; cook, stirring constantly until thick. Correct seasoning if necessary. Pour 1 cup of sauce into 12 × 8-inch baking dish. Reserve ½ cup sauce for top. Add wild rice to sauce remaining in saucepan. Spoon ⅛ of mixture along end of one slice of ham; roll up, place seam-side down in dish. Repeat to make 7 more rolls. Pour remaining sauce over rolls; cover with foil. Bake 25 minutes or until bubbly. Garnish with fluted mushrooms and parsley, if desired.

4 servings.

VARIATION: Add 4 slices crisply fried and crumbled bacon and 2 tablespoons chopped green pepper to filling. Top with ½ cup shredded Cheddar cheese before baking.

Wild Rice Oriental

Try it with chopsticks!

1 cup uncooked wild rice (3 cups cooked)

1 (6-ounce) package sliced ham, cut into
1-inch squares

5 tablespoons vegetable oil

2 eggs

1 tablespoon water

¼ to ½ cup thinly sliced green onions

1 (4-ounce) can mushroom stems and pieces,
drained

Dash of pepper

1 to 2 tablespoons soy sauce

Cook wild rice following one of basic methods (page xvi). In large skillet, sauté ham in 1 tablespoon oil; remove from skillet and set aside. Beat eggs with water. Add 1 tablespoon oil to skillet and cook eggs, turning to cook both sides; remove from skillet and set aside. Cut into narrow strips. In remaining 3 tablespoons oil, sauté wild rice 5 minutes, stirring often. Gently stir in ham, egg strips, onions, mushrooms (chopped, if large) and pepper. Cook about 3 minutes to heat through. Stir in soy sauce.

4 servings.

Baked Pork Chops & Wild Rice

For each serving:
2 to 3 tablespoons uncooked wild rice
1 thick pork chop
Seasoned salt
Pepper
1 (½-inch) thick slice fresh tomato
1 thin slice onion
1 (½-inch) thick ring green pepper
Butter

Rinse and drain wild rice. Partially cook (about 20 minutes) following one of basic methods (page xvi); drain. Trim all fat from chops. Season both sides with seasoned salt and pepper. Brown chops in ovenproof skillet. Top each chop with tomato slice, onion slice and green pepper ring. Mound wild rice in each pepper ring; dot with about ½ teaspoon butter. Cover tightly with foil. Bake at 350°F for 1½ hours. If contents become dry, spoon a little water or tomato juice over each chop.

1 chop per serving.

Stir Fried Wild Rice

⅔ cup uncooked wild rice (2 cups cooked)

3 tablespoons vegetable oil

½ pound pork tenderloin, sliced ¼-inch thick

1 cup sliced celery

1 cup sliced green onion

1 cup sliced fresh mushrooms

1 (8-ounce) can sliced water chestnuts, drained

8 ounces fresh or frozen, thawed snow peas or pea pods

1 tablespoon grated fresh ginger root

1 tablespoon cornstarch

1 tablespoon dry sherry

3 tablespoons soy sauce

½ teaspoon salt

½ cup cashews or sunflower nuts

Cook wild rice following one of basic methods (page xvi). Heat oil in heavy skillet; add pork and stir-fry over high heat 2 minutes until meat is no longer pink. Add celery, green onion, mushrooms, water chestnuts, pea pods and ginger root. Stir-fry 5 minutes over high heat until vegetables are tender-crisp. Toss in wild rice until evenly blended. Mix cornstarch with sherry, soy sauce and salt; add to juices in pan and cook about 1 minute until thickened. Toss mixture together to coat everything with the glaze. Garnish with cashews.

4 servings.

Sausage & Wild Rice Casserole

1 cup uncooked wild rice

1 (14-ounce) package bulk pork sausage

1 green pepper, chopped

1 medium onion, chopped

1 cup chopped celery

1 (4-ounce) jar sliced pimento, drained

1 (4-ounce) jar mushrooms

1 (10¾-ounce) can cream of mushroom soup

1 (10¾-ounce) can cream of chicken soup

½ soup can water

2 ounces (about ½ cup) cheese, shredded

Partially cook wild rice (about 15 minutes) following one of basic methods (page xvi). Brown sausage; add remaining ingredients except cheese. Mix and pour into greased 2-quart casserole; cover. Bake at 350°F for 1 hour. Sprinkle with cheese and bake 15 minutes longer. Add more liquid if necessary.

8 to 10 servings.

Sherried Chicken in Wild Rice Casserole

1 envelope dry onion soup mix

2 cups dairy sour cream

3 (2½- to 3-pound) broiler-fryers

2 cups dry sherry

1 cup water

1 teaspoon salt

Dash of pepper

½ teaspoon dried basil

Pinch of dried thyme

1 teaspoon (or more) curry powder

6 tablespoons minced parsley

1½ cups uncooked wild rice (4½ cups cooked)

1 (10¾-ounce) can cream of mushroom soup

Blend dry soup mix into sour cream; let stand 2 hours. Place chicken in roasting pan; pour sherry and water over chicken. Sprinkle with all seasonings and parsley. Cover roaster. (If lid doesn't fit tightly, place a sheet of aluminum foil over pan before covering.) Bake at 300°F for 1½ hours or until meat falls off bones. Remove chicken from roaster. Cover loosely and set aside to cool. Cook wild rice following one of basic methods (page xvi). Strain pan juices from roaster into saucepan; simmer until reduced to 1½ cups. Gradually blend in mushroom soup until smooth and heat together a few minutes. Slowly combine with sour-cream mixture. The cream will not curdle if blended slowly; pour hot liquid into cream mixture a little at a time. Skin and bone cooled chicken; cut into bite-size pieces. Combine with cooked, drained wild rice and turn into buttered casserole. Pour sauce over chicken and rice; toss lightly. Bake at 300°F for 30 minutes.

12 servings.

Low Calorie Chicken with Wild Rice

⅓ cup uncooked wild rice

4 celery stalks, sliced

1 medium green pepper, diced

1⅓ cups water

2 teaspoons instant chicken bouillon or 2
   chicken bouillon cubes

1 teaspoon salt

2 whole chicken breasts, halved and skinned

Soy sauce

Rinse and drain wild rice. Mix with celery, green pepper, water, bouillon and salt in greased 2-quart casserole. Place chicken on top of rice mixture. Brush with soy sauce; cover. Bake at 350°F for 1½ hours or until rice is tender. Garnish with celery leaves, if desired.

4 servings.

Foolproof Chicken Bake

1 cup uncooked wild rice

1 (10¾-ounce) can cream of celery soup

1 (10¾-ounce) can cream of chicken soup

1 envelope dry onion soup mix

1 soup can dry white wine

3 chicken breasts, halved, skinned and boned

Rinse and drain wild rice. Mix soups, soup mix, wine and wild rice; let stand several hours. Pour into flat casserole. Arrange chicken on top of rice; cover. Bake at 350°F for 1 hour; remove cover, stir and bake 1 hour longer.

6 servings.

VARIATION: Substitute 1 cut-up (2½- to 3-pound) broiler-fryer for chicken breasts. Substitute 2 cups boiling water and 1 (4-ounce) can mushrooms for celery soup, chicken soup and white wine.

Chicken, Wild Rice & Bacon Casserole

1 cup uncooked wild rice (3 cups cooked)

1 pound bacon

4 cups chopped celery

2 large onions, chopped

1 cup chopped green pepper (optional)

4 cups cut up cooked chicken

2 (10½-ounce) cans chicken with rice soup

2 (4-ounce) cans mushrooms, drained

Salt, pepper and garlic powder to taste

Cook wild rice following one of basic methods (page xvi). Dice bacon; fry until crisp. Remove from skillet and reserve enough drippings to sauté celery, onions and green pepper until soft. Combine wild rice, chicken, bacon, vegetables, soup, mushrooms and seasonings in large greased casserole or roaster. Stir carefully to mix well; cover. Bake at 325°F for 45 minutes or until heated through.

8 servings.

Chicken Breasts & Wild Rice

⅓ cup uncooked wild rice (1 cup cooked)
4 chicken breasts, halved and boned
3 tablespoons butter or margarine
¼ cup minced onion
½ cup slivered almonds
1 (4-ounce) can mushrooms
¼ cup chopped pimento
½ (10¾-ounce) can cream of mushroom
    soup
1 cup dairy sour cream
½ cup chicken broth
1 teaspoon salt
½ teaspoon white pepper

Cook wild rice following one of basic methods (page xvi). Brown chicken breasts in butter. Remove from pan; set aside. Brown onion; remove and set aside. Brown almonds. Mix rice, onion, almonds, mushrooms and pimento; place in greased flat baking dish. Place chicken breasts on top. Mix soup, sour cream, broth, salt and pepper; heat until smooth. Pour over chicken. Bake at 325°F for 1 hour.

8 servings.

Sweet-Sour Chicken Wild Rice

2 cups cooked wild rice (²/₃ cup uncooked)

1 (10¾-ounce) can cream of mushroom or cream of chicken soup

1 (13-ounce) can pineapple chunks

3 cups cubed, cooked chicken or turkey

2 tablespoons soy sauce

1 large green pepper, cut into strips

Cook wild rice following one of basic methods (page xvi). Blend soup with pineapple and juice. Add chicken, soy sauce, green pepper and wild rice. Pour into greased 1½-quart casserole. Bake at 325°F for 30 minutes.

4 servings.

Wild Rice & Chicken Liver Pilaf

1 cup uncooked wild rice
1 medium green onion, chopped
1 green pepper, chopped
½ cup chopped celery
½ cup butter or margarine
16 chicken livers, cut in half
½ teaspoon salt
½ teaspoon seasoned salt
¼ teaspoon pepper
3 tablespoons brandy

Cook wild rice following one of basic methods (page xvi). Sauté onion, green pepper and celery in ¼ cup of butter 5 minutes. Remove vegetables from skillet, leaving some butter. Sauté half of livers until light brown; add vegetables and sautéed livers to wild rice and season with salts and pepper. Heat remaining ¼ cup butter in same skillet and sauté remaining livers until lightly browned. Keep rice warm but do not overcook. Heat brandy in a ladle; ignite and pour over livers. Stir until flame goes out. Place rice on warmed plate and add remaining livers on top.

6 servings.

Turkey Wild Rice Supreme

1 cup uncooked wild rice (3 cups cooked)

½ cup chopped onion

½ cup butter

¼ cup all-purpose flour

1 (6-ounce) can broiled, sliced mushrooms or
  1 (4-ounce) can whole mushrooms or
  stems and pieces

1½ cups half-and-half

3 cups diced, cooked turkey

¼ cup diced pimento

2 tablespoons snipped parsley

1½ teaspoons salt

¼ teaspoon pepper

½ cup slivered blanched almonds (optional)

Cook wild rice following one of basic methods (page xvi). In saucepan, sauté onion in butter until tender but not brown; stir in flour. Cook until bubbly. Drain mushrooms; reserve liquid. Add water to measure 1½ cups. Gradually add liquid and cream to onion, stirring constantly until mixture boils; cook and stir 1 minute. Add wild rice, mushrooms, turkey, pimento, parsley, salt and pepper. Pour into greased 2-quart casserole. Sprinkle with almonds. Bake at 350°F for 40 minutes.

8 servings.

VARIATION: White wine can be substituted for ½ cup of the liquid.

Turkey Breast with Wild Rice Stuffing

Wild Rice Stuffing (page 87)

1 boneless turkey breast (about 3 pounds) skinned

2 tablespoons butter or margarine, melted

½ cup dry sauterne

2 teaspoons juniper berries

⅛ teaspoon dried thyme

1 cup whipping cream

1 teaspoon Calvados brandy

Prepare Wild Rice Stuffing. Put turkey breast between sheets of plastic wrap. With flat side of mallet, pound to 12 × 14-inch rectangle, about 1-inch thick. Spoon stuffing lengthwise down center of turkey breast. Using plastic wrap as a guide, pull meat up around stuffing, pressing it firmly into a roll, enclosing stuffing. Tie with string in several places or use "bookbinders" wrap to secure the roll. Brush with melted butter. (If there is any extra stuffing, it can be baked in a casserole for about the last 30 minutes of roasting time.) Place stuffed turkey roll in large baking pan. Heat oven to 325°F. Combine sauterne, juniper berries and thyme. Pour over meat. Roast 45 to 60 minutes until a thermometer inserted in center of turkey roll reads 165 to 170°F. Remove turkey from pan. Remove strings. Keep turkey warm. Degrease pan with cream; spoon out juniper berries. Bring liquids to boil and cook over medium-high heat until reduced by half and slightly thickened. Stir in brandy. To serve, place turkey roll on heated platter and spoon extra stuffing on one side. Spoon sauce over turkey to glaze; serve with remaining sauce.

6 servings.

Wild Rice Stuffing

½ cup uncooked wild rice (1½ cups cooked)

¼ cup butter or margarine

1 cup shredded carrots

½ cup golden raisins

½ cup chopped pistachio nuts, or pine nuts
  or slivered almonds

6 green onions, sliced

1 apple, cored and finely chopped

2 tablespoons lime juice

½ teaspoon freshly ground cardamom

½ teaspoon salt

½ teaspoon freshly ground black pepper

Cook wild rice following one of basic methods (page xvi). Melt
butter in skillet; add carrots, raisins, nuts, onions, apple and lime
juice. Cook over medium-high heat until carrots are done, about
5 minutes. Remove from heat; stir in wild rice. Add cardamom,
salt and pepper.

Kingdom Come Duck

4 wild ducks

2 apples

2 celery stalks

2 (10½-ounce) cans consommé

1 soup can water

1½ to 2 cups uncooked wild rice (4½ to 6 cups cooked)

Sauce (below)

4 slices bacon, crisply fried and crumbled

Stuff each duck with ½ apple and ½ celery stalk. Place duck's breast-down in consommé and water in baking dish. Cover tightly and bake at 350°F for 3 hours. Meanwhile, cook wild rice following one of basic methods (page xvi). Duck should be very tender. Slice breast meat away from bone. Place in greased shallow casserole. Pour Sauce over ducks; cover and bake just until heated through, about 15 minutes. Serve duck breast on a bed of the cooked wild rice; sprinkle with bacon. Pass Sauce.

6 to 8 servings.

Sauce

1½ cups butter

⅔ cup sherry

½ cup bourbon

1 (5-ounce) jar currant jelly

¼ cup Worcestershire sauce

In a saucepan, slowly heat butter, sherry, bourbon, jelly and Worcestershire sauce until well blended and jelly melts. Sauce may be thickened with a little flour or cornstarch, if desired.

Pheasant & Wild Rice

1 cup uncooked wild rice (3 cups cooked)

1 (10¾-ounce) can cream of mushroom soup

⅔ cup whipping cream

4 ounces (about 1 cup) Cheddar cheese, shredded

3 strips bacon, diced

1 onion, finely chopped

½ cup sliced fresh mushrooms

⅓ cup chopped green pepper

½ cup sliced water chestnuts

1 pheasant, cut up

Flour

Shortening

Paprika

Chopped parsley

Cook wild rice following one of basic methods (page xvi). Heat mushroom soup and cream; add cheese. Fry bacon, onion, mushrooms and green pepper; drain. Add to soup mixture. Add water chestnuts. Put wild rice in greased casserole. Roll pheasant in flour; brown in shortening. Put on top of rice and pour cheese mixture over pheasant. Sprinkle with paprika and parsley. Bake at 325°F for 30 to 45 minutes.

4 servings.

Top of the Stove Wild Rice

1½ cups cooked wild rice (½ cup uncooked)
Bouillon
1 small onion, chopped
½ green pepper, chopped
1 stalk celery, diced
1 carrot, finely diced
3 tablespoons butter or margarine
1 cup diced, cooked chicken, beef or shrimp

Cook wild rice in bouillon, following one of the basic methods
page xvi). In large skillet, sauté vegetables in butter until tender.
Stir in wild rice and chicken; heat through.

4 servings.

TIP: Cooked turkey can be substituted for cooked
chicken in any of these casserole recipes.

Wild & Nutty Rice Stuffing

2 cups uncooked wild rice (6 cups cooked)
8 strips bacon
10 green onions, including tops, sliced
2 cups chopped pecans, walnuts or filberts,
    or unsalted sunflower nuts
1 pound fresh mushrooms, sliced

Cook wild rice following one of basic methods (page xvi). Cut bacon into julienne strips; fry in skillet. Add onions, nuts and mushrooms; cook and stir 10 minutes. Stir in wild rice; place in greased casserole; cover. Bake at 350°F for 1 hour.

8 servings.

VARIATION: Amount is sufficient to stuff 12 Rock Cornish hens. If any wild rice mixture remains, it can be wrapped in aluminum foil or put into a greased, covered oven-proof dish and baked with hens at 350°F for 20 to 30 minutes.

Saucy Wild Rice Stuffed Game Hens

⅓ cup uncooked wild rice (1 cup cooked)

2 tablespoons butter or margarine

8 ounces fresh mushrooms, sliced

4 green onions, chopped

2 small pork sausage patties, crumbled

4 Rock Cornish hens, including giblets

1¾ cups chicken stock

¾ cup dry white wine

¼ cup minced parsley

1 teaspoon dried basil

Salt and pepper to taste

Sauce (page 93)

Cook wild rice following one of basic methods (page xvi). Melt butter in saucepan; sauté mushrooms and green onions until soft. Add sausage and sauté about 3 or 4 minutes. Remove mushroom mixture with slotted spoon and set aside. Reduce heat; add chopped giblets, chicken stock, wild rice, wine, parsley and basil. Season with salt and pepper. Cook stuffing until liquid is absorbed. Remove stuffing from heat; stir in ½ of mushroom mixture. Fill hens with stuffing; put in roasting pan, and brush with melted butter. Roast at 375°F for 1¼ hours. Remove hens from pan and keep warm. Degrease pan juices and pour into measuring cup. Add stock if necessary to measure 1 cup; set pan juice aside for Sauce.

4 servings.

Sauce

¼ cup butter or margarine
3½ tablespoons all-purpose flour
1 teaspoon caraway seeds
¾ cup whipping cream
½ cup chicken stock

Melt butter; combine flour and caraway seeds; whisk into butter.
Cook, stirring constantly until frothy and smooth. Whisk in cream
and chicken stock. Add reserved pan juices and remaining half
of mushroom mixture. Cook and stir until smooth. Serve hens
and pass sauce separately.

Duck with Wild Rice Stuffing

½ cup uncooked wild rice (1½ cups cooked)
6 strips bacon, diced
2 stalks celery, minced
1 medium onion, minced
½ green pepper, minced
¼ teaspoon dried oregano
¼ teaspoon pepper
Salt to taste
4 small ducks

Cook wild rice following one of basic methods (page xvi). Fry bacon until crisp; remove from pan and drain. Sauté celery, onion and green pepper in bacon drippings until tender; drain. Combine with bacon, well-drained wild rice and seasonings. Fill cavities of ducks with stuffing and close openings with small skewers. Bake at 325°F for about 3 hours. For crisp ducks, turn oven temperature at 400°F for the last 20 to 30 minutes. Place strips of bacon over breasts of birds if they are not fat enough.

4 servings.

Herbed Wild Rice Stuffing for Turkey

⅔ cup uncooked wild rice (2 cups cooked)

4 teaspoons instant chicken bouillon or 4 chicken bouillon cubes

1 cup chopped celery

½ cup chopped green pepper (optional)

½ cup butter or margarine

1 cup hot water

1 (8-ounce) package herb-seasoned stuffing mix

1 to 2 teaspoons poultry seasoning

12- to 14-pound turkey

Salt and pepper to taste

Melted butter

Cook wild rice following one of basic methods (page xvi), dissolving 3 teaspoons chicken bouillon in cooking water. In medium skillet, cook celery and green pepper in butter until tender. Dissolve remaining bouillon in hot water. In large bowl, combine wild rice, celery, green pepper, stuffing mix and poultry seasoning; mix well. Season turkey with salt and pepper. Stuff neck and body cavities loosely; truss. Place breast-side up on rack in shallow roasting pan. Brush with butter. Roast as turkey label directs or according to your own favorite method. Turn extra stuffing into well-greased 1-quart baking dish; cover and refrigerate. Bake for last 30 minutes of roasting time.

24 to 28 servings.

VARIATION: Add 1 (8-ounce) can sliced water chestnuts, drained, with vegetables.

Stuffing-in-a-Bag for Turkey

½ cup uncooked wild rice (1½ cups cooked)

1 (6½-ounce) package long grain and wild rice mix

2 (4-ounce) cans mushrooms

½ cup margarine or butter

1 large onion, chopped

2 cups chopped celery

1 teaspoon poultry seasoning

Salt and pepper to taste

2 eggs

14-pound turkey

Cook wild rice following one of basic methods (page xvi). Slightly undercook long grain and wild-rice mix, following package directions. Drain mushrooms; reserve liquid for gravy. Melt margarine in skillet; add mushrooms, onion, celery, poultry seasoning, salt and pepper. Cook until onion is transparent. Combine rices and cooked ingredients in large pan; mix in eggs. Refrigerate.

To stuff turkey, cut 2 large squares cheesecloth; insert center of one piece in body cavity and fill with stuffing (a flour scoop works well). Tie corners of cheesecloth together with string. Close bird with poultry pins. Fill neck cavity in same way. Roast as desired. When turkey is done, carefully remove stuffing bags, using oven mitt. Place stuffing in serving bowl. Stuffing can also be used in regular way, or baked in casserole.

28 servings.

Wild Rice, Cranberry & Mushroom Stuffing

For double-thick pork chops, chicken or turkey . . .

²/₃ cup uncooked wild rice (2 cups cooked)

1½ cups finely chopped mushrooms

½ cup chopped onion

3 tablespoons butter or margarine

¼ teaspoon salt

Freshly ground pepper

1 cup chopped fresh or frozen cranberries

⅓ cup currants or raisins (optional)

Cook wild rice following one of basic methods (page xvi). In skillet, over medium to low heat, sauté mushrooms and onion in butter until mushrooms are cooked and dry and onion is soft, about 10 minutes. Add salt, pepper, cranberries, currants and wild rice. Place stuffing in meat; fasten. Bake, broil or barbecue until meat is cooked. Can be baked separately in casserole at 350°F about 30 minutes.

3 cups stuffing; enough for 6 double-thick pork chops.

Wild Rice Mushroom Stuffing

1⅓ cups uncooked wild rice (4 cups cooked)
¼ cup chopped onion
1 cup sliced fresh mushrooms
⅓ cup butter or margarine
½ to 1 teaspoon salt
Dash of pepper

Cook wild rice following one of basic methods (page xvi). Cook and stir onion and mushrooms in butter until brown. Mix with wild rice, salt and pepper. Cool; stuff turkey just before roasting.

Enough for 10- to 12-pound turkey or goose.

Fruited Wild Rice Stuffing

1 cup uncooked rice (3 cups cooked)

½ cup butter or margarine

¼ cup orange juice

1 cup bread crumbs

½ cup raisins

½ cup chopped walnuts

½ cup apple chunks

Cook wild rice following one of basic methods (page xvi). Melt butter; add orange juice. Combine with remaining ingredients and wild rice. Place in greased 2-quart casserole; cover. Bake at 325°F for 1 hour.

1½ quarts; enough for 10-pound turkey.

VARIATION: Can also be used as a bed for baked chicken or turkey breast, or as stuffing for rolled-up chicken breasts.

TIP: Try one of these delicious stuffings in a whole baked fish!

Orange Wild Rice Stuffing

1⅓ cups uncooked wild rice (4 cups cooked)

1 (11-ounce) can mandarin oranges

1 (4-ounce) can mushrooms, drained

⅓ green pepper, chopped

½ small onion, chopped

¼ cup butter or margarine

1 cup chopped celery (optional)

1 (10¾-ounce) can cream of mushroom soup

½ teaspoon salt

½ teaspoon sage

¼ teaspoon pepper

Cook wild rice following one of basic methods (page xvi). Drain mandarin oranges; reserve juice. Sauté mushrooms, green pepper and onion in butter until onion is transparent. Combine remaining ingredients with ¼ cup mandarin orange juice (use remainder of juice in gravy). Mix all ingredients together. Stuff bird just before roasting.

6 cups; enough for a large duck or chicken.

Wild Rice Bacon Stuffing

Size of turkey or chicken	4 pounds	12 pounds	20 pounds
Cooked wild rice (uncooked)	2 cups (²/₃ cup)	6 cups (2 cups)	10 cups (3¹/₃ cups)
Coarse or fine day-old bread crumbs	1 qt	3 qts	5 qts
Bacon*	¹/₂ lb	1 lb	1¹/₂ lbs
Bacon drippings or fat	¹/₄ cup	³/₄ cup	1¹/₄ cups
Onion, chopped	¹/₄ cup	³/₄ cup	1¹/₄ cups
Celery, chopped leaves included	¹/₂ cup	1¹/₂ cups	2¹/₂ cups
Salt*	¹/₂ to 1 tsp	1¹/₂ to 3 tsp	2¹/₂ to 5 tsp
Pepper	¹/₄ tsp	³/₄ tsp	2 tsp
Dried herbs, such as half thyme and half sage, crumbled	1 tsp	1 tbsp	5 tsp
Poultry seasoning	to taste	to taste	to taste

*Or cooked pieces from turkey neck, giblets, etc.; use larger amount of salt called for in recipe if giblets are used.

Cook wild rice following one of basic methods (page xvi). Prepare coarse or fine bread crumbs, as desired. Fry bacon. Remove from skillet; drain on paper towels and crumble. Add onion and celery to skillet. Stir in some of bread crumbs; brown. Turn into deep bowl; mix lightly with remaining ingredients. For dry stuffing, add little or no liquid. For moist stuffing, with fork, lightly mix in enough broth or hot water to moisten dry crumbs. Cool. Place stuffing in turkey just before roasting. Roast as turkey label directs. Bake any extra stuffing in greased casserole during last 30 minutes of roasting time. Bread crumbs can be prepared ahead and frozen. The night before stuffing turkey, measure bread and other dry ingredients. Prepare bacon, celery, onion, etc. Refrigerate ingredients overnight and combine just before stuffing.

Wild Rice Shrimp Bake

¼ cup uncooked wild rice (¾ cup cooked)

½ cup chopped celery

2 tablespoons chopped green onion

2 tablespoons chopped green pepper

½ cup butter

1 (4-ounce) can mushrooms or 1 cup sliced
  fresh mushrooms

1 (4¼-ounce) can shrimp, drained

Soy sauce

Cook wild rice following one of basic methods (page xvi). Brown celery, onion and green pepper in butter. Add wild rice, mushrooms and shrimp. Mix well; pour into greased 1-quart casserole. Bake at 350°F for 30 minutes. Serve with soy sauce.

2 servings.

Minnesota Walleye Cioppino on Wild Rice

1²/₃ to 2 cups uncooked wild rice (5 to 6 cups cooked)

1½ pounds walleye fillets (or lake trout or whitefish)

2 tablespoons olive oil

2 tablespoons butter or margarine

1½ cups sliced onion

2 cloves garlic, minced

1 (28-ounce) can Italian-style plum tomatoes

1 cup dry white wine

1 cup water

2 tablespoons chopped parsley

1 to 1½ teaspoons salt

1½ teaspoons dried basil

½ teaspoon dried oregano

1 pound cleaned, deveined raw shrimp

12 to 16 clams or 1 (8-ounce) can minced clams

2 tablespoons butter or margarine

Cook wild rice following one of basic methods (page xvi). Cut fish into 1-inch chunks; set aside. Heat oil and butter in Dutch oven; add onion and garlic and cook 2 minutes over high heat. Add tomatoes, wine, water, parsley, salt, basil and oregano; heat to boiling. Reduce heat and simmer 30 minutes. Add fish and simmer 10 minutes. Add shrimp and clams and simmer 5 minutes. Serve in individual wide, flat soup bowls. Put wild rice in the bottom and ladle the cioppino mixture over it; top with pat of butter.

6 to 8 servings.

Wild & White Rice Crab Casserole

½ cup uncooked wild rice (1½ cups cooked)

¼ cup uncooked white rice (about ½ cup cooked)

½ cup minced celery

½ small green pepper, minced

½ small onion, minced

12 ounces fresh mushrooms, sliced

2 tablespoons butter or margarine

1 cup frozen or canned crabmeat, drained and flaked

1 (10¾-ounce) can mushroom soup

¼ cup buttered bread crumbs

1 tablespoon shredded Cheddar cheese

White Sauce with Nuts (page 105)

Cook wild rice following one of basic methods (page xvi). Cook white rice following package directions. Meanwhile, sauté celery, green pepper, onion and mushrooms in butter. Mix rices, vegetables, crabmeat and mushroom soup. Put in buttered 2-quart baking dish; sprinkle with crumbs and shredded cheese. Place baking dish in pan of hot water. Bake at 350°F for 50 minutes. Serve with White Sauce with Nuts.

4 to 6 servings.

White Sauce with Nuts

   2 tablespoons butter
   2 tablespoons all-purpose flour
   1 cup milk
   ¼ teaspoon salt
   ¼ teaspoon pepper
   ¼ slivered almonds, toasted

Melt butter; add flour and mix thoroughly. Remove from heat; gradually add milk, stirring constantly. Add salt and pepper. Return to heat; heat to boiling, stirring constantly. Boil and stir 1 minute. Add almonds.

Oysters & Wild Rice en Casserole

1½ cups uncooked wild rice (4½ cups cooked)

½ cup chopped green pepper

¼ cup butter

2 cups sliced fresh mushrooms

1 cup chablis or sauterne

1 teaspoon salt

¼ teaspoon white pepper

2 cups fresh oysters, well drained

¼ cup butter, melted

Cook wild rice following one of basic methods (page xvi). In skillet, sauté green pepper in ¼ cup butter. Add mushrooms, wine, salt and pepper; simmer 15 minutes. Mix with cooked rice; spread in greased shallow 2-quart baking dish. Dip oysters in remaining melted butter and arrange on top of wild rice. Bake at 350°F 30 minutes. Watch oysters carefully so they do not overcook.

6 to 8 servings.

HERB-SEASONED VARIATION: Add 1 clove garlic, minced, 2 tablespoons celery, ½ teaspoon dried oregano, ½ teaspoon dried basil and ½ teaspoon dried marjoram with mushrooms.

Scampi on Wild Rice

An elegant first course . . .

1 cup uncooked wild rice (3 cups cooked)

2 pounds large raw shrimp (about 12 to 15 per pound)

½ cup butter

1 teaspoon salt

6 cloves garlic, crushed

¼ cup chopped fresh parsley

2 teaspoons grated lemon peel

2 tablespoons lemon juice

Lemon wedges

Cook wild rice following one of basic methods (page xvi); keep hot. Remove shells from shrimp, leaving shell on tail section only. Devein; rinse under running water and drain on paper towels. Heat oven to 400°F. Melt butter in 13 × 9 × 2-inch baking dish in oven. Add salt, garlic and parsley; mix well. Arrange shrimp in single layer in baking dish; turn over to butter both sides of shrimp. Bake, uncovered, 5 minutes. Turn shrimp, sprinkle with lemon peel, juice and remaining parsley. Bake 8 to 10 minutes or just until tender. Arrange hot wild rice on individual serving dishes or a heated platter. Arrange shrimp on wild rice, dividing shrimp evenly if making individual servings. Garnish with lemon wedges. Serve immediately.

8 servings.

Seafood & Wild Rice

1⅓ cups uncooked wild rice (4 cups cooked)

8 ounces fresh mushrooms, sliced and sautéed in butter

1 cup chopped celery

1 cup chopped green pepper

1 cup chopped onion

½ cup butter

2 (10¾-ounce) cans cream of mushroom
soup

2 soup cans half-and-half

2 (7-ounce) cans crabmeat

1 (7-ounce) can lobster

1 pound shrimp, cooked

Salt, pepper and cayenne pepper to taste

Slivered almonds

½ cup white wine

Cook wild rice following one of basic methods (page xvi). Sauté
mushrooms, celery, green pepper and onion in butter until soft.
Combine wild rice with remaining ingredients except almonds
and wine, in large casserole. Sprinkle with slivered almonds;
cover. Bake at 350°F for 45 minutes. Pour white wine over
contents of casserole. Bake uncovered 15 minutes longer.

10 to 12 servings.

Seafood Casserole with Shrimp Sauce

⅔ cup uncooked wild rice (2 cups cooked)
½ cup uncooked white rice (1 cup cooked)
1 cup flaked crabmeat
1½ cups chopped celery
1 green pepper, chopped
1 medium onion, chopped
1 (10-ounce) package frozen peas, thawed
1 (2-ounce) jar chopped pimento, drained
3 (10¾-ounce) cans cream of mushroom soup
1 cup broken shrimp
1 pound fresh mushrooms, sliced
2 tablespoons butter

Cook wild rice following one of basic methods (page xvi). Cook white rice following package directions. Combine rices, crabmeat, celery, green pepper, onion, peas and pimento. Add 1½ cans soup and ½ cup shrimp. Place mixture in baking dish. Bake at 350°F for 1 hour.

For sauce, brown mushrooms in butter. Stir in remaining soup and shrimp; heat through. Serve crab and rice mixture with the hot mushroom and shrimp sauce.

8 to 10 servings.

Salmon Supreme

1 cup uncooked wild rice (3 cups cooked)

1 (15½-ounce) can red salmon

1 (10¾-ounce) can cream of chicken soup

½ cup dairy sour cream

5 teaspoons instant minced onion

½ teaspoon dill weed

½ teaspoon salt

¼ teaspoon pepper

1 (10-ounce) package frozen asparagus spears

4 ounces (about 1 cup) medium sharp Cheddar cheese, shredded

Cook wild rice following one of basic methods (page xvi). Drain salmon, reserving liquid. Bone and flake; set aside. Heat soup, salmon liquid, sour cream, onion, dill weed, salt, pepper and wild rice. Fold in salmon. Turn into greased shallow 2-quart baking dish. Bake at 350°F for 15 to 20 minutes. Cook asparagus and drain. Arrange over salmon mixture. Sprinkle with cheese. Bake 15 minutes longer. Garnish with parsley, if desired.

6 to 8 servings.

Wild Rice & Tuna with Almonds Casserole

1 cup uncooked wild rice (3 cups cooked)

2 (10¾-ounce) cans cream of mushroom soup

1 cup chicken broth

1 cup chopped celery

¼ cup chopped onion (optional)

2 tablespoons chopped green pepper

2 tablespoons butter or margarine

1 (4-ounce) can mushrooms

1 tablespoon chopped pimento

Dash of garlic powder

Salt and pepper to taste

1 (3-ounce) package sliced almonds

2 (6½-ounce) cans tuna, drained and flaked

Bread crumbs, buttered

Cook wild rice in chicken broth following one of basic methods (page xvi). Stir soup and broth together until smooth. Combine with remaining ingredients except bread crumbs. Place in greased 1½-quart casserole. Top with bread crumbs. Bake at 350°F for 1 hour.

6 to 8 servings.

VARIATION: Substitute 1 pound cooked shrimp or cut-up cooked chicken for tuna. Sprinkle with shredded cheese before baking.

Tomato Wild Rice Casserole

2 cups uncooked wild rice

2 small onions, chopped

1 (8-ounce) can mushroom stems and pieces,
   or 2 cups fresh mushrooms, sliced

8 ounces Cheddar cheese, shredded or cubed

1 (28-ounce) can whole tomatoes

1 cup pimento-stuffed green olives

½ cup olive, peanut or vegetable oil

Rinse and drain wild rice. Combine with remaining ingredients.
Pour into large greased casserole; cover. Bake at 325°F for 2 to
2½ hours, stirring occasionally.

8 to 10 servings.

Hiawatha Bake

1 cup uncooked wild rice

1 cup shredded or cubed process American, Velveeta or natural Cheddar cheese

1 cup fresh mushrooms, chopped, or 1 (4-ounce) can mushrooms

1 cup ripe or pimento-stuffed olives, chopped

1 cup canned tomatoes

½ cup chopped onion

1 cup hot water

⅓ cup vegetable oil

½ teaspoon garlic salt

Rinse wild rice. Soak overnight in water to cover; drain. Place in greased 2-quart casserole; stir in remaining ingredients; cover. Bake at 350°F for 1 to 1½ hours.

4 to 6 servings.

VARIATION: Omit onion; add 1¼ cups cut-up pepperoni.

Wild Rice Mushroom Crêpes

12 Wild Rice Crêpes (page 169)
3 pounds fresh mushrooms, chopped
2 tablespoons butter or margarine
1 large onion, chopped
2 cloves garlic, minced
¼ cup all-purpose flour
¾ cup half-and-half or whole milk
2 tablespoons dry sherry (optional)
½ cup freshly grated Parmesan cheese
¼ cup chopped parsley
Salt to taste
Dairy sour cream (optional)
Lingonberries (optional)

Prepare crêpes. Sauté mushrooms in butter; add onion and garlic and cook until moisture disappears, about 10 minutes. Stir in flour; cook until bubbly. Gradually add cream and sherry, stirring constantly until mixture boils. Cook and stir 1 minute, until thickened. Add Parmesan cheese, parsley and salt. Divide filling between crêpes and roll up. Place in shallow baking dish. Brush with additional butter and broil until lightly browned. Serve with sour cream and a dollop of lingonberries.

6 servings.

Herb Wild Rice & Cheese Casserole

1 cup uncooked wild rice (3 cups cooked)

¼ cup minced onion

2 tablespoons chopped green pepper

1 (4-ounce) can sliced mushrooms, drained

2 tablespoons butter or margarine

1 (10¾-ounce) can cream of mushroom soup

4 ounces (about 1 cup) Cheddar cheese, shredded

¾ cup half-and-half

¼ teaspoon dried marjoram

⅛ teaspoon dried basil

⅛ teaspoon dried tarragon

½ teaspoon curry powder

½ teaspoon salt

¼ teaspoon pepper

Cook wild rice following one of basic methods (page xvi). Heat oven to 350°F. Meanwhile, sauté onion, green peppers and mushrooms in butter about 5 minutes. Stir in soup, cheese, half-and-half and seasonings. Heat mixture slowly about 10 minutes. Add wild rice to cream sauce mixture. Pour into greased 2-quart casserole. Bake 8 to 10 minutes or until heated through.

8 to 10 servings.

VARIATION: Add ½ cup chopped celery, sautéed with onion; omit herbs; add 1 (8-ounce) can sliced water chestnuts, drained, to cream sauce with wild rice.

Spanish Wild Rice

1½ cups uncooked wild rice

2 cups water

Salt

1 teaspoon butter

1 cup water

1 (6-ounce) can tomato paste

½ cup chopped parsley

1 teaspoon salt

1 teaspoon dried oregano

½ teaspoon dried basil

2 onions, finely chopped

½ cup finely chopped green pepper

2 cloves garlic, minced

½ cup crisply fried, crumbled bacon

1 (28-ounce) can whole tomatoes

Cook wild rice in 2 cups water with butter and salt about 20 minutes; drain. Combine 1 cup water and tomato paste; stir in parsley and seasonings. Combine wild rice, onions, green pepper, garlic, bacon and tomato-paste mixture. Add tomatoes (which have been mashed or broken up). Pour into greased 3-quart casserole; cover. Bake at 325°F for 1½ hours.

8 to 10 servings.

Wild Rice with Pasta, Herbs, Tomatoes & Cheese

3 medium tomatoes, peeled, seeded and
diced

4 cloves garlic, minced

1/2 cup chopped fresh parsley

1/2 cup chopped fresh (or 2 tablespoons
dried) basil

1 tablespoon fresh mint, chopped

3/4 teaspoon salt

1/2 teaspoon freshly ground black pepper

1/4 teaspoon hot pepper flakes

1/2 cup olive oil

2/3 cup uncooked wild rice (2 cups cooked)

2 cups water

3/4 teaspoon salt

1 (10-ounce) package spinach noodles

1/2 cup freshly grated Parmesan cheese

8 ounces Fontina cheese, shredded (about 2
cups)

In medium bowl, toss tomatoes, garlic, parsley, basil, mint, 3/4
teaspoon salt, black pepper, pepper flakes and olive oil. Let stand
at room temperature 30 minutes to 4 hours to blend flavors.
Rinse wild rice in hot tap water; drain. Cook following one of
basic methods (page xvi). While rice cooks, cook noodles following package directions until *al dente*. Mix wild rice with tomato
mixture. While noodles are still warm, blend with cheeses. Turn
into large shallow dish. Top with wild rice mixture. Serve at room
temperature.

6 servings.

Canadian Bacon & Wild Rice Quiche

⅓ cup uncooked wild rice (1 cup cooked)

1 small onion, diced

⅓ cup julienne strips of Canadian bacon

9-inch unbaked pie shell

4 ounces (about 1 cup) Monterey Jack cheese, shredded

3 eggs

1½ cups half-and-half

½ teaspoon salt

Dash of Tabasco sauce

Cook wild rice following one of basic methods (page xvi). Fry onion and Canadian bacon together until onion is translucent; drain. Spread onion and bacon in pie shell. Add cheese and cooked wild rice. In mixing bowl, whip eggs, half-and-half, salt and Tabasco together. Pour over wild rice. Bake at 350°F for 50 minutes or until knife inserted near center comes out clean. Cut into wedges; serve with cranberry sauce, if desired.

5 to 6 servings.

VARIATION: Can be baked in 13 × 9 × 2-inch pan (line bottom of pan with pastry). Cut into small squares or slices for appetizers.

Wild Rice Filling for Omelets

⅓ cup uncooked wild rice (1 cup cooked)
1 tablespoon chopped red pepper
1 tablespoon chopped green pepper
1 tablespoon finely chopped onion
2 tablespoons butter or margarine
Ham bits (optional)
Sunflower nuts (optional)

Cook wild rice following one of basic methods (page xvi). Sauté red and green pepper and onion in butter 2 to 3 minutes over medium heat. Stir in wild rice. Heat thoroughly. Add cooked, chopped ham bits and sunflower nuts. Fill omelets just before folding.

Filling for six 2-egg omelets.

Breads

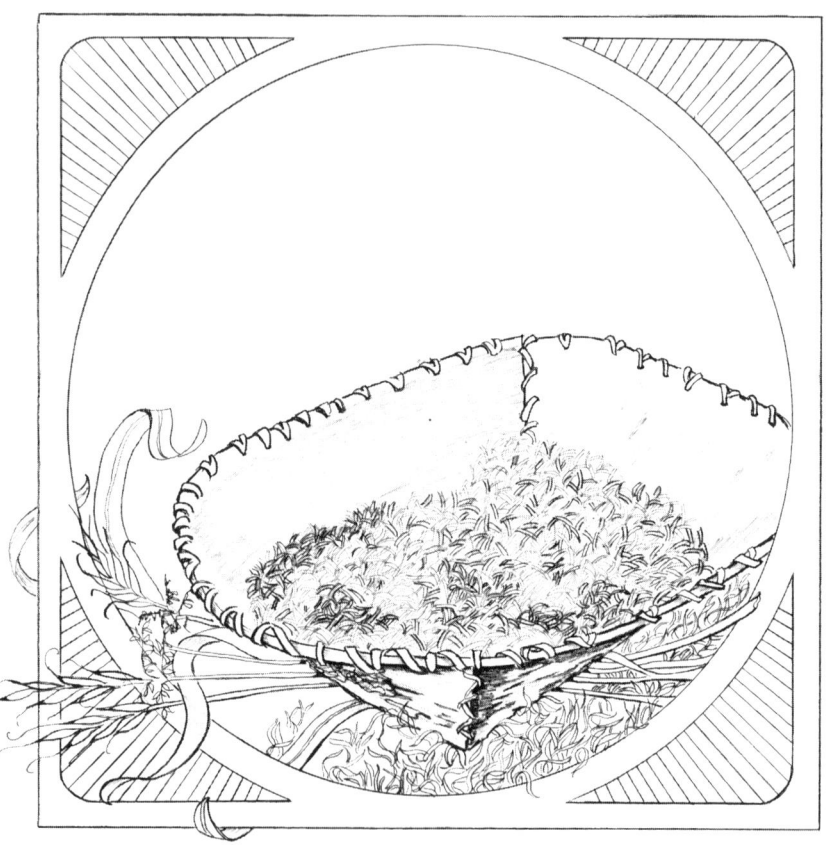

Winnowing is the final step in separating the good grain from the chaff. This is done by gently tossing or shaking the rice from a birch-bark tray called a winnowing basket, allowing the wind to carry off the light chaff and the clean grain to drop to a blanket below.

Wild Rice Bread Stalks

Not just for fun, these bread sticks are snipped to resemble wild rice stalks as they grow in the bogs. Stand them up in a crock or basket for a showy presentation on a buffet table.

⅓ cup uncooked wild rice (1 cup cooked)

1½ cups warm water (105 to 115°F)

1 package active dry yeast

1 tablespoon sugar

2 teaspoons salt

¼ cup vegetable oil

½ cup dark rye or pumpernickel rye flour

3½ to 4 cups all-purpose or bread flour

1 egg white, beaten

1 tablespoon water

Coarse salt

Cook wild rice following one of basic methods (page xvi). Combine wild rice, water, yeast, sugar and 2 teaspoons salt in bowl. Stir to blend; let stand 5 minutes until yeast foams. Stir in oil and rye flour; stir in all-purpose flour 1 cup at a time until mixture is stiff. Let rest 15 minutes. Heat oven to 375°F. Turn mixture onto lightly floured surface; divide into 16 pieces. (First divide into quarters, then divide each quarter into 4 parts.) Roll each piece of dough to make a rope 16 to 20 inches long, depending on length of cookie sheet. Place ropes on well-oiled cookie sheets, spacing them well apart. Roll sticks in oil to cover them completely. With scissors, snip about ⅓ of the length of each stick on both sides to resemble the grain on stalks. Beat egg white with 1 tablespoon water; brush on stalks. Sprinkle with coarse salt. The "stalks" may be bent for a more effective presentation on a buffet table. Bake 20 to 30 minutes until browned and crisp. Remove from cookie sheet. Cool on wire rack.

16 stalks.

Blueberry & Wild Rice Muffins

A real Minnesota-grown production . . .

⅓ cup uncooked wild rice (1 cup cooked)

1 cup milk

⅓ cup margarine or butter, melted

2 eggs

1½ cups all-purpose flour

¼ cup packed brown sugar

3 teaspoons baking powder

1 teaspoon ground coriander

1 teaspoon salt

1 cup fresh, frozen or canned, drained blueberries

Cook wild rice following one of basic methods (page xvi); cool. Heat oven to 400°F. Grease 12 (2½-inch) muffin cups. Combine wild rice, milk, margarine and eggs in bowl. Stir flour, brown sugar, baking powder, coriander and salt together; stir into wild-rice mixture just until flour is moistened. Fold in blueberries. Spoon ⅓ cup of batter into each muffin cup. Bake 20 to 25 minutes until tops are golden. Remove from pans immediately. Cool on wire rack.

12 large muffins.

VARIATION: Substitute 1 teaspoon grated lemon peel for coriander; bake in tiny muffin pans 15 to 20 minutes.

24 to 30 tiny muffins.

Gitchi Gumi Fry Bread

*A quick bread that is fried in a shallow pan of oil, typical of
Indian Fry Breads.*

⅓ cup uncooked wild rice (1 cup cooked)

2 cups all-purpose flour

1 cup cornmeal

1 tablespoon baking powder

¾ teaspoon salt

1 cup milk

Oil for deep-frying

Cook wild rice following one of basic methods (page xvi); cool.
Blend flour, ¼ cup of cornmeal, baking powder, salt and wild
rice. Stir in milk until dough is stiff. Divide into four parts; knead
slightly to make smooth balls. Sprinkle board with remaining
cornmeal; roll each part to about 10-inch circle (or diameter of
skillet to be used). Heat oil in skillet to smoking hot, about 400°F.
Carefully lower bread into oil. Fry about 45 to 60 seconds on
each side, until just golden and center is cooked through. Remove
from oil; drain on paper towels. Repeat for each remaining bread.
Serve hot, sprinkled with powdered sugar, if desired. Tear apart
or cut in wedges.

4 breads.

ᴡ𝑖𝑙𝑑 ᴿ𝑖𝑐𝑒 𝑆𝑐𝑜𝑛𝑒𝑠

⅓ cup uncooked wild rice (1 cup cooked)

2½ cups all-purpose flour

5 tablespoons sugar

2 teaspoons baking powder

½ teaspoon baking soda

½ teaspoon salt

½ cup cold butter

⅓ cup buttermilk

2 eggs

Cook wild rice following one of basic methods (page xvi); cool. Heat oven to 400°F. Measure flour, sugar, baking powder, soda and salt into mixing bowl or work bowl of food processor fitted with steel blade. Cut in butter until mixture resembles coarse crumbs (with food processor, 8 to 10 on/off turns). Mix wild rice, buttermilk and eggs. Reserve 1 tablespoon of this mixture. Pour remaining liquid mixture over dry ingredients. Mix just until dry ingredients are blended and dough is soft (with food processor, 6 to 8 on/off turns). Turn dough onto lightly floured surface. Shape into ball and place on ungreased cookie sheet. Roll or pat into a circle 8 inches in diameter. Brush dough with reserved egg-milk mixture. Sprinkle with sugar. With straight knife, cut circle into 8 wedges leaving wedges in place and circle intact. Bake 20 to 25 minutes until golden. Remove from cookie sheet; cool on wire rack. Pull wedges apart to serve.

8 scones.

Wild Rice & Whole Wheat Quick Bread

2 cups whole-wheat flour
1 teaspoon baking soda
½ teaspoon salt
½ cup cooked wild rice
2 tablespoons honey
1 cup buttermilk or plain yogurt
1 egg, beaten

Heat oven to 350°F. Combine dry ingredients in bowl; stir in wild rice. Stir honey, buttermilk and egg together; stir into dry ingredients. Knead 3 to 5 minutes, but do not overmix. Shape into flat, round loaf, about 8 inches in diameter. Place on lightly greased cookie sheet. Make two parallel cuts on top of loaf. Bake 25 to 30 minutes or until toothpick inserted in center comes out clean. Remove from cookie sheet; cool on wire rack.

1 loaf.

VARIATION: Add ½ cup raisins, 1 tablespoon sugar and ¾ teaspoon cinnamon with flour.

Wild Rice & Pecan Waffles

⅓ cup uncooked wild rice (1 cup cooked)

1 cup all-purpose flour

1 teaspoon baking powder

¼ teaspoon salt

2 eggs, separated

⅔ cup milk

¼ cup vegetable oil

½ cup chopped pecans

Cook wild rice following one of basic methods (page xvi); cool. Heat waffle iron. Stir flour, baking powder and salt together; set aside. Beat egg yolks, milk and oil together in medium bowl. Stir in flour mixture just until smooth. In small bowl, beat egg whites until stiff but not dry. Gently fold egg whites into batter until just combined. Stir in pecans and wild rice. For each waffle, pour about ½ cup batter into center of waffle iron, until it spreads to 1 inch from edge. Bake until waffle iron stops steaming. Waffle should be golden. Repeat with remaining batter. Serve hot with butter and syrup, if desired.

4 to 6 waffles.

TIP: Some of the quick-bread recipes call for only small amounts of cooked wild rice. Plan ahead for these and other similar recipes by cooking enough wild rice to refrigerate or freeze for later use.

North Country Wild Rice Pancakes

⅓ to ⅔ cup uncooked wild rice (1 to 2 cups
    cooked)

2 eggs

1½ cups milk

3 tablespoons vegetable oil

1 cup all-purpose flour

3 teaspoons baking powder

1 tablespoon sugar

1 teaspoon salt

Cook wild rice following one of basic methods (page xvi); cool.
Combine eggs, milk and oil in bowl. Stir dry ingredients together;
stir into eggs and milk. If batter is too thick, add more milk.
Pour batter onto hot lightly greased griddle. Sprinkle 1 to 2
tablespoons wild rice on each pancake; cook until dry around
edges. Turn and cook until golden brown. Serve with butter and
syrup, if desired.

16 to 18 pancakes.

TIP: Try sprinkling wild rice on pancakes made
from your own favorite recipe or mix, too.

Mushroom & Wild Rice Pancakes

⅔ cup uncooked wild rice (2 cups cooked)

8 ounces fresh mushrooms, coarsely chopped

2 tablespoons grated onion

¼ cup butter or margarine

3 eggs, beaten

¼ cup milk

1 cup all-purpose flour

2 teaspoons baking powder

1 teaspoon salt

Cook wild rice following one of basic methods (page xvi). Sauté mushrooms and onion in butter. Combine remaining ingredients; stir in mushrooms and onion. If batter is too thick, add more milk. Drop batter onto hot greased griddle; cook until edges are dry. Turn and cook until light golden brown.

12 pancakes.

Wild Rice Buttermilk Pancakes

$^{1}/_{3}$ cup uncooked wild rice (1 cup cooked)

4 eggs

1$^{1}/_{4}$ cups buttermilk

$^{1}/_{2}$ teaspoon baking soda

1$^{1}/_{4}$ cups all-purpose flour

1 teaspoon baking powder

1 teaspoon sugar

$^{1}/_{2}$ teaspoon salt

2 tablespoons butter or margarine, melted

Cook wild rice following one of basic methods (page xvi); cool. Whisk eggs, buttermilk and soda together in large bowl. Combine flour, baking powder, sugar and salt; add to egg mixture. Whisk in melted butter and wild rice. Pour batter onto hot, greased griddle. Cook until dry around edges; turn and cook on other side. Serve with butter and warm fruit or maple syrup, if desired.

16 thin pancakes.

VARIATION: For thicker pancakes, use only 2 eggs.

Sour Cream Pancakes

½ cup cooked wild rice

2 cups unbleached or whole wheat flour

2 teaspoons baking powder

2 teaspoons salt

1 teaspoon baking soda

2 eggs

1 cup dairy sour cream

1 cup milk

2 tablespoons vegetable oil or melted butter

2 tablespoons honey

Chop wild rice in food processor or blender; set aside. Stir dry ingredients together in bowl. Beat eggs in separate bowl; stir in sour cream and milk. Gradually add to dry ingredients. Beat after each addition to make smooth, thin batter. Stir in oil, honey and wild rice. If batter is too thick, add more milk. Pour about ¼ cup batter onto hot oiled griddle. Cook until dry around edges. Turn and cook on other side until light brown. Serve with butter and syrup, if desired.

15 to 18 pancakes.

Mahnomen Rye Bread

¼ to ½ cup uncooked wild rice

2 cups hot water

5 tablespoons brown sugar

2 tablespoons lard or shortening

1 package active dry yeast

¼ cup warm water (105 to 115°F)

2 teaspoons salt

1½ cups rye flour

About 5 cups all-purpose flour

5 tablespoons dark molasses

2 eggs, beaten

Rinse and drain wild rice. Pour hot water over wild rice; cover. Let stand for several hours or overnight. Drain; reserve liquid. Add water, if necessary, to measure 2 cups. Heat 1 cup of liquid with brown sugar and lard, just until lard melts; cool. Dissolve yeast in ¼ cup warm water in large bowl. Add cooled mixture, salt, remaining 1 cup rice liquid, rye flour and 1 cup all-purpose flour. Stir until smooth. Stir in molasses, eggs and wild rice. Add enough additional all-purpose flour to make soft dough. Turn onto lightly floured surface; knead 7 to 8 minutes until smooth. Place in greased bowl; turn to grease top. Cover; let rise in warm place about 1½ hours until double. Punch down; divide dough into halves. Shape into loaves. Place each loaf in greased 9 × 5 × 3-inch pan. Let rise until double. Heat oven to 350°F. Bake 50 to 60 minutes until brown and loaf sounds hollow when tapped. Remove from pans; brush tops with butter. Cool on wire rack.

2 loaves.

Wild Rice & Cracked Wheat Bread

⅔ cup uncooked wild rice (2 cups cooked)

3 packages active dry yeast

¾ cup warm water (105 to 115°F)

½ cup packed brown sugar

½ cup mashed potato flakes

½ cup molasses

½ cup vegetable oil

1 cup wheat germ

1 cup cracked wheat

2 tablespoons salt

6 to 8 cups all-purpose flour

Cook wild rice following one of basic methods (page xvi). Drain and save any liquid. Add water to measure 2½ cups. Dissolve yeast in ¾ cup warm water in large bowl. Add brown sugar, potato flakes, molasses, oil, wheat germ, cracked wheat, salt and 2 cups flour; mix until smooth. Add wild rice and enough of remaining flour to make soft dough. Turn onto lightly floured surface; knead about 5 minutes. Place dough in greased bowl; turn to grease top. Cover; let rise in warm place about 1½ hours until double. Punch down; divide dough into 4 parts. Shape into 4 loaves. Place each loaf in a greased 9 × 5 × 3-inch pan. Let rise until double. Heat oven to 350°F. Bake about 40 minutes until brown and loaf sounds hollow when tapped. Remove from pans; brush tops with butter. Cool on wire rack.

4 loaves.

Pioneer Molasses Bread

½ cup uncooked wild rice (1½ cups cooked)
1 package active dry yeast
¼ cup warm water (105 to 115°F)
½ cup dark or light molasses
¼ cup packed brown sugar
¼ cup vegetable oil or butter, melted
¼ cup instant potatoes or potato flakes*
1 tablespoon salt
7 to 8 cups bread flour

*1 cup leftover mashed potatoes can be substituted for instant potatoes.

Cook wild rice following one of basic methods (page xvi). Drain and save any liquid; add water to measure 2½ cups. Dissolve yeast in ¼ cup warm water in large bowl. Add liquid, molasses, brown sugar, oil, potatoes, salt and 2 cups flour; mix well. Beat until smooth. Add drained wild rice and enough remaining flour to make soft dough. Turn onto well-floured surface; knead about 5 minutes. Place dough in greased bowl; turn to grease top. Cover; let rise in warm place about 2 hours until double. Punch down; let rise 1 hour. Punch down; divide dough into 3 parts. Shape into 3 loaves. Place each loaf in greased 8½ × 4½ × 2¾-inch pan. Let rise about 1½ hours or until double. Heat oven to 375°F. Bake 45 to 50 minutes until brown and loaves sound hollow when tapped. Remove from pans; brush with butter. Cool on wire racks.

3 loaves.

Oatmeal Health Bread

⅔ cup uncooked wild rice (2 cups cooked)

2 cups water

1 cup rolled oats

½ cup molasses

¼ cup butter or margarine

2½ teaspoons salt

½ cup cold water

¾ cup nonfat dry milk powder

1 package active dry yeast

½ cup warm water (105 to 115°F)

5 to 5½ cups all-purpose flour

Cook wild rice following one of basic methods (page xvi). Heat 2 cups water to boiling in saucepan; stir in oats. Cook 1 minute; remove from heat. Stir in molasses, butter, salt, cold water and dry milk; cool to lukewarm. Dissolve yeast in ½ cup warm water; add to oat mixture. Add 3 cups flour; beat well. Stir in wild rice and enough flour to make soft dough. Let rest 10 minutes. Turn onto lightly floured surface; knead until smooth. Place dough in greased bowl; turn to grease top. Cover; let rise in warm place until double. Punch down; divide dough into 3 parts. Shape into 3 round loaves. Place on lightly greased cookie sheets. Let rise until double. Heat oven to 350°F. Bake about 45 minutes until golden and loaves sound hollow when tapped. Remove from cookie sheets; brush tops with butter. Cool on wire racks.

3 loaves.

Wild Rice and Three Grain Bread

1/3 cup uncooked wild rice (1 cup cooked)

1 package active dry yeast

1/3 cup warm water (105 to 115°F)

2 cups milk, scalded and cooled

1/2 cup honey

2 tablespoons butter or lard, melted

2 teaspoons salt

1/2 cup rolled oats

1/2 cup rye flour

2 cups whole-wheat flour

About 4 cups bread or all-purpose flour

1 egg, beaten

1 tablespoon water

1/2 cup sunflower nuts, plain or salted

Cook wild rice following one of basic methods (page xvi). Dissolve yeast in warm water in large bowl. Stir in milk, honey, butter and salt. Stir in oats, rye flour, whole-wheat flour and 2 cups of the bread flour. Stir in wild rice. Cover dough; let rest 15 minutes. Stir in enough remaining flour to make stiff dough. Turn onto lightly floured surface; knead 10 minutes until smooth, adding more flour as necessary to keep dough from sticking. Place dough in greased bowl; turn to grease top. Cover; let rise in warm place about 2 hours until double. Punch down; knead briefly on lightly oiled board. Shape into one of the following:

- One large free-form loaf. Place on lightly greased cookie sheet.
- Divide into 3 parts; shape into strands and braid. Place on lightly greased cookie sheet in wreath or other desired shape.

- Divide into 2 parts, shape into loaves. Place in lightly greased 9 × 5 × 3-inch pans.
- Divide into 4 parts; shape into oblong French-bread-type loaves. Place on lightly greased cookie sheets.

Let rise about 45 minutes until double. Heat oven to 375°F. Combine egg and water; brush on tops of loaves. Slash long loaves if desired. Sprinkle with sunflower nuts. Bake 45 minutes or until loaf sounds hollow when tapped. Remove from pans. Cool on wire racks.

1 large loaf, or 1 wreath, or 2 pan loaves
or 4 French-bread-type loaves.

Side Dishes

Today, many brands and grades of wild rice appear in specialty shops and grocery stores in burlap bags, crocks and boxes.

Wild Rice with Mushrooms & Almonds

*By far the most popular way to serve wild rice is as a side dish,
judging from the many who sent in this recipe and its countless
variations....*

1 cup uncooked wild rice

½ cup slivered almonds

2 tablespoons chopped green onions or
chives

¼ cup butter or margarine

3 cups chicken broth

1 (8-ounce) can mushrooms, drained

Rinse and drain wild rice. In large skillet, cook and stir almonds
and onions in butter until almonds are golden. Pour wild rice
into greased 1½-quart casserole. Heat broth to boiling; stir into
wild rice. Stir in almonds, onions and mushrooms. Cover tightly
and bake at 325°F for 1½ hours or until liquid is absorbed and
rice is fluffy.

6 to 8 servings.

VARIATIONS

- Brown wild rice with almonds and onions before adding broth.
- Substitute bacon drippings for butter to brown the almonds and onions.
- Other ingredients which can be added: 1 clove garlic, minced, or ½ teaspoon dried thyme, or ¼ cup chopped green pepper (sauté with onion), or ½ cup coarsely chopped or sliced ripe olives or ¼ cup chopped celery.
- Substitute 3 chicken or beef bouillon cubes or 3 teaspoons instant bouillon dissolved in 3 cups water for chicken broth.
- Substitute ½ cup dry white wine for ½ cup of the chicken broth.
- Substitute 1 (10¾-ounce) can cream of mushroom soup for 1 cup of the chicken broth.
- Substitute 2 (10¾-ounce) cans cream of mushroom, 2 (10¾-ounce) cans cream of celery and 2 (10½-ounce) cans chicken with rice soup for the chicken broth.
- Substitute 1 (10¾-ounce) can French onion soup and 1 soup can water for 2 or 3 cups of the chicken broth.
- Use ½ cup wild rice and ½ cup pearl barley for 1 cup wild rice, or ⅓ cup barley, ⅓ cup white rice and ⅓ cup wild rice; use 1 (4-ounce) can mushrooms and omit almonds.
- Cook in heavy saucepan on top of the stove 30 to 45 minutes; add 1 (2-ounce) jar chopped pimento, drained, and ¼ cup minced parsley just before serving.

Creamy Herbed Wild Rice

Delicious alone or serve as a bed for Rock Cornish hens or other poultry.

1 cup uncooked wild rice (3 cups cooked)

1 (8-ounce) can sliced mushrooms, drained

¼ cup minced onion

2 tablespoons minced green pepper

2 tablespoons butter or margarine

1 (10¾-ounce) can cream of mushroom soup

1 cup cream

½ teaspoon curry powder

½ teaspoon salt

¼ teaspoon pepper

¼ teaspoon dried marjoram

⅛ teaspoon dried basil

⅛ teaspoon dried tarragon

Cook wild rice following one of basic methods (page xvi). In large skillet, sauté mushrooms, onion and green pepper in butter for about 5 minutes. Stir in soup, cream and seasonings; heat 10 minutes. Add wild rice and heat through, stirring occasionally.

4 servings.

Apple Cider & Wild Rice Medley

Goes well with pork chops or ham . . .

1 cup uncooked wild rice

1 1/4 cups apple cider or cranapple juice

1 1/4 cups water

1/2 cup butter or margarine

1/2 cup almonds, coarsely chopped

1/2 cup golden raisins

Cinnamon (optional)

Nutmeg (optional)

Rinse and drain wild rice. Combine with cider and water in large kettle. Heat to boiling; reduce heat, cover and simmer 50 to 60 minutes, stirring gently during last 15 minutes of cooking time. Remove from heat. In large skillet or electric fry pan, melt butter; blend in almonds and raisins and cook gently 5 minutes. Blend in cooked wild rice. Season with cinnamon and/or nutmeg.

6 servings.

Wild Rice Nokomis

1¼ cups uncooked wild rice
3 cups water
¾ cup sliced celery
¾ cup chopped onion
2 tablespoons butter or margarine
1 (10¾-ounce) can beefy mushroom soup

Rinse wild rice; soak in fresh cold water 6 hours or overnight; drain. Sauté celery and onion in butter; add rice and soup. Pour into greased 1½-quart casserole; cover. Bake at 350°F for 40 minutes.

6 servings.

Herbed Wild Rice

1 cup uncooked wild rice

3 cups boiling water

3 beef or chicken bouillon cubes or 3 teaspoons instant bouillon

$\frac{1}{2}$ teaspoon salt

$\frac{1}{4}$ teaspoon dried thyme

$\frac{1}{4}$ teaspoon dried basil

$\frac{1}{3}$ cup chopped onion

$\frac{1}{4}$ cup butter or margarine

12 ounces fresh mushrooms, sliced

Rinse wild rice; soak 30 minutes and drain. In double boiler over hot water, combine rice, boiling water, bouillon cubes, salt, thyme and basil. Cook 45 minutes. Sauté onion in butter; add mushrooms and more butter if needed, to brown them. Combine with wild rice; pour into greased 1½-quart casserole; cover. Bake at 350°F for 20 to 25 minutes.

6 to 8 servings.

Baked Herbal Wild Rice

1 cup uncooked wild rice
1 onion, finely chopped
1 teaspoon dried chervil
1 teaspoon dried basil
1 teaspoon dried tarragon
1/8 teaspoon freshly ground pepper
1/4 cup butter
2 1/2 cups boiling chicken broth

Rinse and drain wild rice. Combine with remaining ingredients and place in 1 1/2-quart casserole. Cover and bake at 350°F for 1 1/2 hours. Stir gently with fork after 1 hour.

4 to 6 servings.

Wild Rice Tomato Combo

1 cup uncooked wild rice
½ pound bacon, cut up
1 medium onion, chopped
1 cup chopped celery
½ cup finely chopped green pepper
1 (16-ounce) can tomatoes
2 (8-ounce) cans tomato sauce
1 (4-ounce) can mushroom stems and pieces
10 pimento-stuffed olives, sliced
Potato chips (optional)

Rinse wild rice; cover with water and soak several hours or overnight. Heat to boiling; reduce heat, cover and simmer 20 minutes. Drain. Partially fry bacon; add onion, celery and green pepper. Sauté until transparent. Add tomatoes and tomato sauce; heat to slow boil. Add mushrooms and olives; simmer at least 1 hour. Drain wild rice, combine with sauce. Turn into greased casserole. Bake at 350°F for 30 to 40 minutes. Top with crushed potato chips.

6 servings.

Baked Barley with Brown & Wild Rice

Wild rice combines happily with other grains to make a hearty, easy-to-prepare side dish for meat, fish or poultry.

⅓ cup uncooked wild rice

⅓ cup pearl barley

⅓ cup brown rice

2 tablespoons butter or margarine

1 clove garlic, minced

1 large sweet onion, sliced into ¼-inch rings

8 ounces fresh mushrooms, sliced

3 cups beef or chicken broth

1 teaspoon dried thyme

Salt and pepper to taste

Rinse wild rice in hot tap water; drain. Combine with barley and brown rice. In heavy, 2-quart casserole, heat butter and garlic; sauté 1 minute. Add grains and sauté 2 to 3 minutes until shiny, stirring often. Add onion, mushrooms, broth and thyme. Bake, covered, along with meat or poultry, at 300°F for 2½ hours, or at 350°F for 1 hour. Add salt and pepper to taste.

6 servings.

TIP: Part white rice or part pearl barley can be used in place of some of the wild rice in most side-dish and main-dish recipes. The proportions can vary as long as the total amount is the same as is called for in the recipe.

Nutty Wild Rice

1 cup uncooked wild rice
5 1/2 cups chicken stock or water
1 cup pecan halves
1 cup golden raisins
1/4 cup chopped fresh mint
4 green onions, thinly sliced
Grated peel of 1 large orange
1/3 cup fresh orange juice
1/4 cup olive oil
1 1/2 teaspoons salt
Pepper, freshly ground

Rinse and drain wild rice. Place in medium-size, heavy saucepan. Add stock and heat to boiling; reduce heat and simmer 45 minutes. Check for doneness after 30 minutes; rice should not be too soft. Place thin towel inside colander and turn rice into colander to drain. Place wild rice in bowl; add remaining ingredients and toss gently. Season to taste. Let stand at least 2 hours to allow flavors to develop. Serve at room temperature.

6 servings.

Bemidji Bake

2 cups uncooked wild rice
¼ cup chopped green onion
⅓ cup butter or margarine
1 cup sliced fresh mushrooms
2 medium tomatoes, diced
½ cup slivered almonds
¼ cup diced cooked bacon
¼ teaspoon dried thyme
¼ teaspoon dried oregano
⅛ teaspoon saffron
4½ cups chicken broth

Rinse and drain wild rice. Sauté onion in butter; add rice and stir well. Place in greased 3-quart casserole with mushrooms, tomatoes, almonds, bacon, seasonings and broth; cover. Bake at 325°F for 1 hour. Uncover and bake 15 minutes longer.

8 servings.

Old Settlers' Wild Rice

1 cup uncooked wild rice

1/2 teaspoon salt
1 cup whipping cream
1/2 cup chopped onion

Rinse and drain wild rice; place in top of double boiler. Fill top and bottom of double boiler with boiling water. Cover and let stand overnight (do not cook). Drain rice if necessary. Add salt to cream. Layer wild rice, onion and cream in greased 1½-quart casserole; cover. Bake at 350°F about 40 minutes or until onion is cooked.

6 to 8 servings.

TIP: Stir-ins for Cooked Wild Rice: *Use your imagination to dress up plain cooked wild rice. Check your pantry shelves and leftovers in the refrigerator for possible additions. To 4 cups cooked wild rice add:*

- 2 tablespoons unsalted butter, 3 chopped dried apricots, 2 tablespoons chopped filberts, 1/2 teaspoon kosher salt, and freshly ground pepper to taste.
- 2 cups sliced celery and 2 cups chopped onions, stir-fried to tender-crisp, 3 tablespoons soy sauce and salt and pepper to taste.

Wild Rice Ring with Mushroom Sauce

2 cups uncooked wild rice (6 cups cooked)

5 teaspoons instant chicken bouillon or 5 chicken bouillon cubes

1/2 cup hot water

1/3 cup butter or margarine, melted

2 tablespoons all-purpose flour

Mushroom White Sauce (page 153)

Cook wild rice following one of basic methods (page xvi). Dissolve bouillon in water. Melt butter; stir in flour until thoroughly blended; gradually add bouillon and water. Heat to boiling; cook and stir 1 minute. Add to wild rice and mix well. Press into greased 6-cup ring mold. Can be refrigerated at this point for later baking. Bake at 350°F over pan of hot water (or cook in steamer) 40 to 60 minutes. Unmold on serving platter and decorate with parsley, if desired. Serve with Mushroom White Sauce.

6 to 8 servings.

Mushroom White Sauce

    1 to 1½ cups sliced fresh mushrooms

    2 tablespoons butter

    2 tablespoons all-purpose flour

    2 cups milk

    2 chicken bouillon cubes or 2 teaspoons
        instant bouillon

Sauté mushrooms in butter until limp; stir in flour. Cook over low heat, stirring until mixture is bubbly. Gradually add milk and bouillon cubes. Heat to boiling, stirring constantly. Boil and stir 1 minute.

Mushrooms & Artichokes in a Wild Rice Ring

4 chicken bouillon cubes, or 4 teaspoons instant chicken bouillon

4½ cups boiling water

⅓ cup uncooked wild rice

1⅓ cups uncooked white rice

½ cup butter or margarine, melted

Mushroom-Artichoke Filling (page 155)

Grease 5-cup ring mold. In medium saucepan, dissolve bouillon cubes in boiling water. Add wild rice; simmer, covered, 25 minutes. Add white rice; simmer, covered about 20 minutes longer or until rices are tender. Drain if necessary. Mix in butter. Spoon into prepared ring mold; press down with back of spoon. Set aside 5 minutes. Invert onto serving platter. Spoon Mushroom-Artichoke Filling in center of ring.

6 to 8 servings.

Mushroom-Artichoke Filling

12 ounces fresh mushrooms

4 tablespoons butter or margarine

1 (8½-ounce) can whole artichoke hearts

3 tablespoons all-purpose flour

1 cup chicken broth

½ cup water

1 teaspoon lemon juice

½ teaspoon lemon peel

1 teaspoon paprika

¼ teaspoon pepper

Clean mushrooms and cut into halves (makes 4 cups). In large skillet, melt 2 tablespoons of the butter. Add mushrooms and sauté until golden, about 5 minutes. Remove with slotted spoon and set aside. Drain artichoke hearts, reserving ¾ cup of the liquid. Cut artichokes into quarters; set aside. Melt remaining 2 tablespoons butter; mix in flour. Cook over low heat, stirring until mixture is bubbly. Gradually stir in chicken broth, water and artichoke liquid; heat to boiling. Cook and stir 1 minute. Mix in lemon juice and peel, paprika, pepper, reserved artichokes and mushrooms. Cook and stir until vegetables are heated through, about 2 minutes.

Wild Rice Ring·a·Ling

An attractive side dish—try it filled with a bright, colorful vegetable for variety!

1 cup uncooked wild rice (3 cups cooked)
1 pound fresh mushrooms
¼ cup butter or margarine

Cook wild rice following one of basic methods (page xvi). Clean mushrooms. Remove stems; reserve caps. Grind or chop stems and sauté in butter 5 minutes. Blend with wild rice. Pour into greased 4-cup ring mold. Set mold in pan of hot water. Bake at 350°F for 30 minutes. Unmold onto platter. Sauté mushroom caps in butter and serve in center of ring.

4 to 6 servings.

Wild Rice with Bacon

2 cups uncooked wild rice (6 cups cooked)
6 strips bacon, cut up
2 stalks celery, diced
1 medium onion, diced
½ green pepper, diced
1 (8-ounce) can sliced mushrooms, drained
1 (2-ounce) jar chopped pimento, drained
Dash of sage
Salt and pepper to taste
Celery salt and/or seasoned salt to taste (optional)

Cook wild rice following one of basic methods (page xvi). Fry bacon until crisp; remove from skillet and set aside. Add celery, onion, green pepper, mushrooms and pimento to bacon drippings in skillet; cook until celery is tender-crisp. Add wild rice and sage; season to taste. Heat through. Add bacon just before serving.

12 to 14 servings.

Ratatouille with Wild Rice

Super-simple dish for a crowd! A great accompaniment for
barbecued or roasted lamb or beef, or served as
a vegetable main dish.

$^2/_3$ cup uncooked wild rice

2 cups chicken broth

$^3/_4$ cup olive oil or vegetable oil

2 medium green peppers, sliced

8 ounces fresh mushrooms, sliced

1 cup thinly sliced onion

2 cloves garlic, crushed

3 medium zucchini, sliced diagonally, $^1/_4$-inch
thick

1 medium eggplant, quartered lengthwise,
sliced $^1/_4$-inch thick

4 medium tomatoes, peeled, cut into wedges

1 to 2 teaspoons salt

$^1/_4$ teaspoon pepper

$^1/_4$ cup chopped parsley

Rinse wild rice with hot tap water. In saucepan, heat rice and chicken broth to boiling. Cover and simmer 30 minutes or until broth is absorbed. Heat ¼ cup of oil in large skillet, over high heat. Sauté green peppers, mushrooms, onion and garlic 5 minutes or until onion is transparent. Place in large bowl. Add 2 tablespoons of oil to skillet and, over high heat, sauté zucchini until tender, about 5 minutes. Add to vegetables in bowl. Sauté eggplant, turning occasionally, until tender, about 5 minutes. Return vegetables to skillet. Add cooked wild rice and half of tomato wedges. Sprinkle with salt, pepper and 1 tablespoon parsley. Stir to combine. Place in serving dish; top with remaining tomato wedges and sprinkle with remaining parsley. Serve hot or at room temperature.

14 to 16 servings.

Wild Rice with Currants

A one-step method with an unusual flavor...

⅔ cup uncooked wild rice

3 cups whole milk, scalded

½ cup currants

Bouquet garni (½ teaspoon dried thyme, 1 bay leaf, 2 sprigs parsley)

Salt and pepper to taste

Rinse and drain wild rice. Place in top of double boiler over hot water. Pour milk over wild rice. Add currants, bouquet garni (tied in cheesecloth bag or put in tea ball), salt and pepper. Cook, covered, until wild rice is tender and milk has been absorbed, about 1½ hours. Remove bouquet garni before serving.

6 to 8 servings.

Wild Rice, Broccoli & Cheese Casserole

An excellent vegetarian main dish ...

- ²/₃ cup uncooked wild rice (2 cups cooked)
- 1 (20-ounce) package frozen chopped broccoli
- ¹/₂ cup butter or margarine
- ¹/₂ cup chopped celery
- ¹/₄ cup chopped onion
- 1 (8-ounce) can sliced water chestnuts, drained
- 8 ounces (about 2 cups) Colby or Monterey Jack cheese or combination, shredded
- 1 (10³/₄-ounce) can cream of mushroom soup

Cook wild rice following one of basic methods (page xvi). Cook broccoli until tender-crisp; drain. Melt butter; add celery and onion and cook until tender-crisp. Set aside. Grease 1¹/₂-quart casserole. Layer half of wild rice, half of broccoli, half of water chestnuts and half of cheese (save a little for topping) in casserole. Repeat layers; pour on mushroom soup and sprinkle celery and onions over all. Top with reserved cheese. Cover and bake at 350°F for 35 minutes; remove cover and bake 15 minutes longer.

4 to 6 servings.

Old Fashioned Wild Rice & Corn Pudding

A filling combination . . .

⅓ cup uncooked wild rice (1 cup cooked)

1½ cups fresh whole-kernel corn, or 1 (10-ounce) package frozen corn, thawed and well-drained

3 eggs, well beaten

2 tablespoons minced onion

¼ cup all-purpose flour

1½ teaspoons salt

¼ teaspoon white pepper

1 tablespoon sugar

Dash of nutmeg

2 cups half-and-half

2 tablespoons butter, melted

1 (2-ounce) jar chopped pimento, drained

Cook wild rice following one of basic methods (page xvi). In large bowl, combine wild rice, corn, eggs and onion; mix well. Combine flour, salt, pepper, sugar and nutmeg. Stir into corn mixture. Add half-and-half, butter and pimento; mix well. Pour into greased 2-quart shallow baking dish. Set dish in larger pan and pour hot water to 1-inch depth around dish. Bake at 325°F for 1 hour or until pudding is firm and knife inserted in center comes out clean. Cut into squares. Serve hot.

8 servings.

Cauliflower & Carrots with Wild Rice

2 cloves garlic, minced

1 tablespoon butter or margarine

2 cups water

2 teaspoons instant chicken bouillon or 2
   chicken bouillon cubes

1/2 cup uncooked wild rice

1/2 teaspoon salt

1/2 teaspoon onion salt

1/2 cup uncooked white rice

1 cup small fresh caulifiowerets

2 medium carrots, shredded

3 green onions, including tops, thinly sliced

2 to 3 tablespoons whipping cream

Sauté garlic in butter in large saucepan. Add water, bouillon, wild rice and salts; heat to boiling. Reduce heat; cover and simmer 25 minutes. Add white rice; cover and simmer about 20 minutes longer. Add cauliflower; cover and continue to simmer about 10 minutes, until all liquid is absorbed. Stir in carrots, green onions and cream. Heat through over low heat.

6 servings.

Snow Pea & Wild Rice Stir-Fry

1 cup uncooked wild rice

2 green onions, minced

1 tablespoon butter or margarine

2 cups chicken broth

2 tablespoons vegetable oil

4 ounces fresh mushrooms, sliced

1 (8-ounce) can sliced water chestnuts, drained

1 pound snow peas

Salt to taste

¼ teaspoon pepper

1 tablespoon minced parsley

¼ cup whole toasted almonds

Rinse wild rice; drain. In medium saucepan, sauté onions in butter. Add wild rice and broth. Heat to boiling; reduce heat, cover and simmer 35 minutes or until liquid is absorbed. Heat oil in skillet. Sauté mushrooms and water chestnuts quickly. Cook snow peas 2 to 3 minutes in boiling water. Add salt and pepper. Gently combine rice with vegetables, parsley and almonds; serve immediately.

8 servings.

Microwave Wild Rice & Vegetable Platter

⅔ cup uncooked wild rice (2 cups cooked)
4 ounces fresh mushrooms, sliced
Salt to taste
Assorted fresh vegetables such as:
   1 bunch broccoli
   1 head cauliflower
   1 pound carrots
   2 medium zucchini
¼ cup butter or margarine, melted
¼ cup sliced green onions
1 teaspoon dried tarragon

Cook wild rice following one of basic methods (page xvi); cool. Blend wild rice with mushrooms; add salt. Set aside. Prepare vegetables; remove flowerets from broccoli and cauliflower (reserve remainder for another use such as for purée); slice, julienne or shred carrots, cut zucchini into slices or sticks. Arrange broccoli and cauliflower around outside edge of round glass or other microwave-safe platter. Make inner circle of carrots, then zucchini slices. Fill center with mound of wild-rice and mushroom mixture. Drizzle with butter and sprinkle with green onions, tarragon and salt. Cover with plastic wrap. Refrigerate until ready to cook. Slit plastic wrap; microwave on high power 10 to 12 minutes or until vegetables are tender-crisp.

6 servings.

Desserts

Some call it the caviar of grains; others, soul food of the north. However you serve it, you'll be telling your family and guests they are special by including wild rice on the menu.

Cinnamon Wild Rice Pudding

⅔ cup uncooked wild rice (2 cups cooked)

2 cups hot half-and-half

½ cup maple syrup

2 eggs

1 teaspoon vanilla

¾ cup golden or dark raisins

½ teaspoon cinnamon

¼ teaspoon nutmeg

Cinnamon-sugar

Cook wild rice following one of basic methods (page xvi). Heat oven to 350°F. Combine half-and-half, maple syrup, eggs, vanilla, raisins, cinnamon, nutmeg and wild rice. Turn into a 1½-quart casserole. Sprinkle with cinnamon-sugar. Bake 1 hour or until pudding is set. Serve warm or chilled.

8 to 10 servings.

Wild Rice Crepes with Berries

12 Wild Rice Crêpes (below)
1 to 2 tablespoons lingonberry preserves, or
   ¼ cup fresh raspberries or strawberries
Whipped cream

Spread each crêpe with lingonberry preserves, raspberries or strawberries. Top with rounded spoonful of whipped cream. Roll up and top with additional whipped cream.

6 servings.

Wild Rice Crepes

3 eggs
½ cup cold milk
½ cup cold water
¼ teaspoon salt
1 cup all-purpose flour
½ cup cooked wild rice
Butter or margarine

Whisk eggs, milk, water, salt, flour and wild rice together in a bowl. Let batter rest 30 minutes. Heat crêpe pan until drop of water sizzles on surface; lightly butter pan. Cook crêpes, using ⅓ cup batter for each one. Stack finished crêpes between pieces of waxed paper.

Makes about 16 crêpes.

Apple-Wild-Rice Betsy

⅓ cup uncooked wild rice (1 cup cooked)

3 cups peeled and sliced cooking apples (about 3)

⅓ cup packed brown sugar

¼ cup rolled oats

1 tablespoon all-purpose flour

½ teaspoon cinnamon

3 tablespoons butter or margarine softened

Cook wild rice following one of basic methods (page xvi); cool. Place half of apple slices in 1½-quart greased casserole. Combine wild rice with remaining ingredients until crumbly. Sprinkle half of mixture over apples; repeat layers. Bake at 350°F for 25 to 30 minutes or until apples are tender. Serve warm or cool, topped with whipped or regular cream, if desired.

4 servings.

Glorified White & Wild Rice Dessert

⅓ cup uncooked wild rice (1 cup cooked)

1 cup cooked white rice

2 cups drained crushed pineapple

1 cup miniature marshmallows

¼ cup halved maraschino cherries

1 cup whipping cream

¼ cup powdered sugar

1 teaspoon vanilla

Cook wild rice following one of basic methods (page xvi); chill. Combine rices, pineapple, marshmallows and cherries. Just before serving, whip cream with powdered sugar and vanilla; fold into fruit-and-rice mixture.

10 servings.

Creamy Wild Rice Ambrosia

1 cup uncooked wild rice (3 cups cooked)

1 (20-ounce) can pineapple chunks, drained

1 (11-ounce) can mandarin oranges, drained

1 (3-ounce) jar maraschino cherries, drained and halved

1 cup broken walnuts

1 cup miniature marshmallows

1 cup flaked coconut

1 cup whipping cream, whipped, or 1 (9-ounce) carton frozen whipped topping, thawed

1 (4-serving) package lemon pudding, prepared and cooled

Cook wild rice following one of basic methods (page xvi); cool. Combine with fruit, nuts, marshmallows and coconut. Combine whipped cream and pudding; fold into wild rice-fruit mixture. Turn into serving dish. Refrigerate at least 1 hour before serving.

12 to 14 servings.

Apricot & Wild Rice Dessert

¾ cup uncooked wild rice

2 cups water

¾ cup apricot brandy

6 ounces dried apricots, cut up

1 cup whipping cream

2 tablespoons sugar

Sliced almonds

Cook wild rice in water and brandy over medium heat until rice is tender and beginning to pop open, about 45 minutes. Drain if necessary; chill. Just before serving, whip cream with sugar. Fold apricots and wild rice into cream. Garnish with almonds.

6 to 8 servings.

Wild Rice Ice Cream Topping

⅓ cup uncooked wild rice (1 cup cooked)

1 cup evaporated milk

¼ cup butter or margarine

2 cups packed brown sugar

⅛ teaspoon salt

¼ teaspoon maple flavoring or vanilla

½ cup coarsely chopped walnuts

½ cup coarsely chopped maraschino cherries

Cook wild rice following one of basic methods (page xvi). Combine milk, butter, brown sugar and salt. Heat to boiling over low heat, stirring constantly. Continue boiling slowly, stirring occasionally, until it becomes smooth and the consistency of thick cream. Add flavoring, nuts and cherries; fold in well-drained wild rice. (Chopped dates and raisins can be added for variety.) Cool and serve over ice cream, spice cake or bread pudding.

About 8 servings.

Wild Rice Fancy

½ cup uncooked wild rice (1½ cups cooked)

½ cup packed brown sugar

½ cup chopped dates

½ cup chopped pecans

½ cup halved maraschino cherries

Whipped cream

Cook wild rice following one of basic methods (page xvi); chill. Combine with brown sugar, dates, pecans and cherries. Serve topped with whipped cream. Make early in the day to let the flavors blend.

3½ cups; 4 to 6 servings.

Wild Rice Crunch

1 pound uncooked wild rice (8 to 10 cups
   cooked)

1 pound brown sugar

4 cups raisins

1 (16-ounce) jar dry roasted peanuts

Cook wild rice following one of basic methods (page xvi); chill.
Combine with remaining ingredients. Serve over yogurt, ice cream,
pudding or custard. Refrigerate in covered container up to 2
weeks; freeze for longer storage.

4 quarts.

Some Wild Rice Sources

The following are supporters of the Minnesota Wild Rice Council. Write or call these companies for information on quantity purchases and prices.

DEERWOOD RICE &
GRAIN PROCESSING
Route 1, Box 2
Deerwood, MN 56444
(218) 534-3762

DEER RIVER WILD RICE
PROCESSING
PO Box 296
Deer River, MN 56636
(218) 246-2713

F AND S FARMS
John or Dick Florhaug
Box 68
Keliher, MN 56650
(218) 647-8601

GIBBS WILD RICE, INC.
Route 2
Deer River, MN 56636
(218) 246-8505

MacGREGOR WILD RICE
COMPANY
PO Box 288
Aitkin, MN 56431
(218) 927-2219

MILLE LACS WILD RICE
PO Box 200
Aitkin, MN 56431
(218) 927-2740

NORTHWESTERN WILD
RICE COMPANY
965 Payne Avenue
St. Paul, MN 55101
(612) 774-0353

RAY PUETZ
Route 1, Box 60
Brainerd, MN 56401
(218) 829-8058

SARA BAY COMPANY
Arden Plaza, Suite 180
3585 North Lexington
Avenue
St. Paul, MN 55126
(612) 483-5469

UNITED WILD RICE, INC.
402 11th Street SE
Grand Rapids, MN 55744
(218) 326-0571

Contributors

Special thanks to all who contributed recipes, tested and tasted or helped in a variety of other ways. Because of you, this book has become a reality.

Mrs. James H. Anderson
Judy Anderson
Lillian Anderson

Patricia Donovan Baker
Elaine Baldrica
Gladys Barron
Vivian Bartsch
Donna Bassett
Mrs. Alton S. Berg
Sandy Berger
Larry Berle
Mary S. Bever
Ty Birkeland
Mrs. Clifford Bird
Ethel Blanchard
JoAnn Blanchard
Amelia Bresson
Gertrude Breyer
Byerly's

Ailia E. Carlson
Laura Chelesnik
Harriet Chez
Toy Clark

Alice Dahl
Shirley Dayton
Marilyn Denny
Donna DeRusha
Marilyn Dickel
Mildred Dolliff
Norma Hayer Dolliff
Pat Dolzeal
Ann Donight
Beth Dooley
Evelyn B. Dooley

Clover Earl
Kathryn Ebert
Janice Eckman
Mrs. Robert Egerman
Grace Ehlers
Thomas F. Ellerbe, Jr.
Mary Erickson

Ellen Farnham
Jack Farrell
Cecy Faster
Maria Field

Maureen Flahaven
Ardene Flynn
Cyndy Fremling

Gibbs Wild Rice
Millie Gignac
Kay Gillmer
Sherry Glass
Lola D. Glendenning
Mary Grandprey
Mrs. Vern Grover
Daisy Gullat
Gordon E. Gunther
Betsy Guthmann

Douglas A. Hall
Arlene Hallberg
Mrs. Daniel Hanlon
Maxine Harkness
Alice Harrington
Mrs. Edward Haryn
Marian Hedstrom
Kathy Hendrickson
Peggy Henninger
Mrs. Charles Hoyt
Marlys Hruska
Margaret Hubbs

Judy Infelise

Carol E. Jackson
Ruth A. Jacobs
Mrs. Albert A. Jacobson
Helen Jacobson
Gail Javorina
Mrs. A. C. Johnson

Barbara Johnson
Lois Jordan
Mrs. Irwin Jorshaw

Elwilda Kadous
Bev Kaiser
Dorothybelle M. Kaufman
Lois Kennel
Mona Ketzebach
Mrs. M. Lynn Kilibarda
Naomi Kind
Eilleene Kinney
Betty R. Klein
Janie Knier
Ruth Knutson
Betty L. Kosbou
Pat Koski
Irene D. Kriedberg
Marcia Krollman
Beverly Kruse
Cecilia Kutz

Juliana Perlt Lansing
Janet Parsons Larson
Iantha LeVander
Vonnie Lietzau
Sharon Litynski
Mary Elizabeth Love
Jeanette Ludcke
Marnie Luknic
Barbara Lund

Kay MacKenzie
Luella E. Maki
Julia Malnar
Christina Marsolek

Ann Maslow
Maureen McKasy-Donlin
Mildred K. McCabe
Kathleen McKillop
Ruth McMahon
Mrs. Alta M. Miernicki
Eleanore Miller
Glenn Miller
June Miller
Marian Milner
Lois Misner
Lois Molden
Betty Moore
Dorothy Moore
Margaret Moore
Ellie Motter
Joanne Murphy
Eileen Boyce Murray

Gloria Nankervis
Helen Marie Nash
Koreen Neiman
Ilene Nelson
Lauretta Nelson
Lois Nelson
Marie Nelson
Esther Norha
Betsy Norum

Douglas Oaks
Alvina O'Brien
Joan K. O'Brien
Jodell M. O'Connell
Dorothy O'Connor
Elaine Ogren
Beatrice Ojakangas

Ilene Olson
Hazel Olstad
Margaret M. Ordway

Marjorie Pagel
Joy Parker
Mrs. B. W. Parsons, Jr.
June Paulson
Mrs. Julius Perlt
Lola Perpich
Medora Petersen
Betty Peyton
Susan Poupore
Gladys M. Preston
David Prosser
Margaret Prosser

Gretchen Quie

Nancy Rademacher
Donna Ranallo
Maymie Rauvola
Eleanor Reid
Mrs. John Reimann
Dorthy Rickers
Gerald S. Robinson
Lou Romens
Maymie Rowala
Marie Skol Rozycki
Ethelyn Rupp

Mrs. William C. Shacht
Veretta Schedin
Mrs. L. H. Schlauderaff
Mrs. S. M. Shepard
Agnes B. Sherman

Catherine Shikonya	Jan Unger
Earle Sieveling (*New York Cuisine*)	
Sally Simundson	Marion Votel
Bradley Skarich	
Vivian Snyder	Gladys Watkins
Bernice O. Spicer	Mrs. Bob Weber
Judy Stuthman	Mary Wells
Doris Swanson	*Wild Rice for All Seasons Cookbook*,
Mrs. Gerald Swanson	by Beth Anderson
	Sheri Wolfe
Nancy Tetrick	Joyce Wrobleski
Henrietta Theis	
Joan Tilton	Evelyn Young
Patti Tome	Nila Youngren
Richard Tretsven	
Shirley Tretsven	Sue Zelickson

COOKBOOK COMMITTEE

Recipe Editor	Betsy Norum
Editorial Director	Sue Zelickson
Recipe Testing Coordinators	Cecy Faster Helen Jacobson
Illustrator	Mary M. McKee

Index